HIM WE DECLARE

HIM
WE
DECLARE

By
CUTHBERT BARDSLEY
Bishop of Coventry

and

WILLIAM PURCELL
Canon of Worcester

WORD BOOKS—WACO, TEXAS

Printed in Great Britain by
A. R. Mowbray & Co Ltd in the City of Oxford
7121

First published in 1967
Second impression 1967

First American Printing
September 1968

Library of Congress Catalog Card Number: 68-31105
Printed in The United States of America

Contents

v

ACKNOWLEDGEMENTS

THE THANKS of the authors and publishers are due to the following for permission to quote extracts:

Messrs. W. Collins & Co. Ltd., *The Christian Experience of the Holy Spirit* by H. Wheeler Robinson, *The Christian Witness in an Industrial Society* by Horst Symanowski, *Letters and Papers from Prison* by D. Bonhoeffer; Messrs. Harper & Row, Inc., *Christian Outlook* by K. S. Latourette; Messrs. Faber & Faber, *A Grief Observed* by C. S. Lewis, *Four Quartets* by T. S. Eliot; Messrs. Hodder & Stoughton, *New Testament Christianity* by J. B. Phillips, *This Is My Story* and *Woodbine Willie. A Biography* by · William Purcell; Messrs. Longmans, Green & Co. Ltd., *The Fruits of the Spirit* by Evelyn Underhill; Messrs. James Nisbet & Co. Ltd., *Strangers and Pilgrims* by W. R. Matthews; Oxford University Press, *The Idea of the Holy* by Rudolph Otto; Lutterworth Press, *Church and People in an Industrial City* by E. R. Wickham; Messrs. Weidenfeld & Nicolson, *The Protestant Mystics* by Anne Freemantle.

In a list such as this there are bound to be omissions since the authors are indebted to so many on whom they have consciously or unconsciously drawn, but to all of whom—acknowledged or unacknowledged—they wish to express their heartfelt gratitude.

1. A Time to Speak

'TO EVERYTHING,' says the writer of Ecclesiastes, 'there is a season.' There 'is a time to be born, and a time to die; a time to plant, and a time to pluck up that which is planted.' He goes on to include, in a memorable list of those many human activities for which there is the opportune moment, a time to keep silence, and a time to speak. This book arises from the fact that the two men jointly concerned in the writing of it have concluded that, for them at least, the time to speak has come.

What they have to say, moreover, is directed towards a particular kind of men and women who, for a whole variety of reasons, feel that belief in a personal God in an increasingly impersonal world is becoming difficult to the point of impossibility. So this book is not for those whose Christian faith survives intact, undented and, indeed, undaunted by the many pressures to which all faith is now subject. Nor is it for those with a built-in animosity to any religious view of things whatever. Nor is it again for the very considerable number who cannot see that 'religion' matters at all, at any rate so long as they are riding high upon the tide of life. But it is for those, to be in a moment particularized, who really do yearn, even if inarticulately, for 'that faith which gives substance to our hopes, and makes us certain of realities we do not see,'[1] in other words, for faith, for an interpretation of life which gives to the whole experience of living a dimension transcending the purely material. These are

[1] Hebrews 11. 1.

I

they who would like to feel that belief in God who, in Christian terminology, sent his Son into the world, that through him men might believe, is still meaningful, in spite of the many elements in modern life which seem to strike at the roots of such a concept. The essence of the matter is contained, in fact, in the one question as to whether it is possible to know that Christ personally now.

If a personal faith, based upon encounter with this Jesus, no longer seems to be recognizably contemporary experience, then clearly the faith which for two thousand years has existed in his name ought in all honesty to be relegated to a past which a dramatically changing and developing present renders increasingly meaningless, in spite of whatever intellectual arguments may be produced in support of the Christian position in general. The writers of this book believe, however, that Christ is met with now. And since such a belief can only be sustained, not by argument so much as by evidence, they propose, as far as may be, to concentrate on the latter, speaking of Christ in people's lives, more than of anything else.

But they do wish here at the very beginning to particularize further about the kind of people for whom specifically this little book is intended. They are not easy to categorize, because there are so many of them of all ages; and they are to be found in all manner of places and, indeed, in all periods of time. They could be called, and will henceforth in these pages be called, the Quiet People—a term chosen because it seems to identify their most marked characteristic—an inarticulateness concerning matters which might broadly be called spiritual, as distinct from purely material concerns, issues involving life's meaning and purpose, upon which they feel deeply.

There are, furthermore, as it seems to us, two kinds of Quiet People. The first are those within the Church—with an ingrained reverence for its ways and teaching nonetheless real, if not productive of any very startling spiritual experiences. Almost any public affirmation of belief is difficult for them—a further characteristic, and not necessarily an admirable one. 'It is the curse of most good Christians in this country,' wrote R. Ellis Roberts in his biography of Dick Sheppard, 'that they hug their religion as if it were a private matter. The sad saying of that noble Christian, Dr. Johnson, that no sensible man tells his religion, contradicted though it was by its author in every serious sentence and in many public actions, has been given a kind of sacred authority by Englishmen.' Perhaps because of this reserve, these Quiet People often give an impression of a superficial conformity which conceals surprising depths of loyalty, devotion and persistence. And always, in the last resort, those qualities will be found to be directed, not so much to any institution or its representatives, but to Christ himself.

The second kind, or type of Quiet People, as the title is here used, belongs to that indeterminate yet large body who find serious difficulties, intellectual and other, in accepting either what the Church has to say to them now, or disappointment in the fact that what it has to say seems so little, and its manner of doing it so unattractive. These are they who want to believe; but find the going hard. These are they who, if asked to vote on whether they believed in God, would place a cross in the affirmative square, and then wonder wistfully if they had been honest. These are they who are like the man Mark writes of who brought his epileptic son to Jesus, and who, when he saw him healed, could only cry out 'I do believe;

A*

help me to believe more.' He, it may be observed, had
already been to the disciples and got no joy before ever
he brought his trouble to the Lord. Only when that
encounter had taken place did a living faith become
possible. So for this second kind of person we are thinking
of the possibility at least of such an encounter is surely of
importance. And if it is often the only form of Christian
evidence which arouses his respect there is a good warrant
for that.

Now both these kinds of people—and they include the
younger as well as the older—share at least one thing in
common; the experience of having either their faith,
or their seekings after one, put to exceptional strains today.
Why that should be so is an involved matter, and leads, if
its trail be followed, to unprofitable diagnosis. Suffice it
for the moment to say that, while it was never easy to
believe in God, there are grounds for claiming that it is
often at present very difficult indeed.

And now let us try to see these people a little more
clearly. Here, for instance, are four memories of Quiet
People of the first kind, Christians practising a faith
unpretentious yet very real.

The first was a woman who kept a small draper's shop
in a home counties town. A bell pinged whenever the
shop door was opened from the road. An inner door
would open, revealing briefly a room beyond which was,
in fact, the only downstairs accommodation apart from
the shop itself. The opening of this inner door would also
reveal the woman herself. Hers was an undistinguished
face, framed in wispy grey hair. The dentures never
seemed to fit very well; she was very small, with a slight
curvature of the spine. Upstairs lived an invalid sister,
the focus of a great deal of anxiety.

Such an establishment could of course be paralleled in many places. The only indication of anything noteworthy in the situation whatever was a certain look, a certain mounting gleam in the eyes of this woman at the mention of her faith, or anything connected with it. And what was her faith? It was a profoundly felt, built-in conviction of the close presence of Christ. True, for her he was very much the Christ of Galilee, the neighbourhood Christ who could be encountered by the lakeside talking with the fishermen, and very little the mysterious, cosmic, Johannine Christ. He was even, if the truth be told, a rather sentimental Christ, for this woman was a sentimental person, just as this is no doubt a sentimental account of her. But of his reality, of his love, of the fact that, in some odd way, he knew all about her, and meant just what he said in the invitation 'Come unto me, all whose work is hard, whose load is heavy: and I will give you relief' she had no doubt whatever.

This simple faith of hers found its focus in an unattractive church not far down the road. Situated between a brewery and a gasworks it smelt strongly of both, and the brass tablets in it were discoloured. The beauty of holiness was markedly lacking in this uninspiring place. Yet there, year after year, in fair weather and foul, against, as well as with the grain of inclination, with staggering devotion and discipline, she worshipped God in the Christ who at all times and in all places, she felt to be close indeed. To pray with her was an experience in itself; the hem of a garment brushed near: it was possible to feel very close to the reality which, surely beyond all else, has enabled the Christian faith to survive so long. Through what particular channels this grace came to her was never clear: the outstanding fact was its presence. What is more, it overflowed into the whole of her life, making of what would otherwise have been an existence ordinary to the point of banality, limited and enclosed to the point of triviality, something strangely memorable to those who had the good fortune to come in contact with it for awhile. Finally, like the Master she served with such simplicity, this woman had, at the end, to pass through a dark valley. The sister died; she herself, before her own going, became lonely and old, and perhaps failed by those whom she trusted, and who should have served her better. Yet it was not the least of the many unconscious virtues of her life that she left behind in one person at least an abiding sense of the reality of the unseen world and the conviction that the Christ whom she served welcomed her into it.

Another type was a soldier whom many knew in the years following the second world war. Here was a man; stern, uncompromising, straight as a blade, who commanded men. The centurion in the gospels, who asked Jesus to order that his servant be healed, would probably instinctly have come to attention at the sight of him. (Indeed, if by this time they have encountered each other in that bourn from which no traveller returns, he maybe has.) So the soldier was a formidable figure, whom none took lightly. Naturally enough, his Christian faith expressed itself through the traditional, if old-fashioned virtues of the profession of arms: directness, trust, discipline: a willingness to obey as well as to command. Christ had made certain promises. They would be honoured: he was to be obeyed. It was all on record, for men to see and understand. The soldier, in fact, was a Bible Christian, one of many in a long military line of such. To read his Bible daily, to say his prayers, to go to

church, to be a man under authority, were of the essence
of a faith, which certainly had powerful effects upon a
memorable character. He was sixty-three when he died,
calmly confident of meeting an only son who had been
killed in action some years before. His funeral service,
in a London church, drew the captains and the kings.
When it was over, and the traffic flowed by again, some
of those standing around talking of the man to whom
they had thus bidden farewell, were put in mind of the
words:

> He nothing common did, or mean.
> Upon that memorable scene.

It was characteristic therefore of the kind of Christian
this soldier was that he met his Lord in the Word. The
Scriptures stood at the centre of his faith. In this respect
he stands in sharp contrast to a certain woman—another
of the Quiet People—remembered from the early years of
the second world war, who met the Lord in the Sacrament.

The district, industrial South London, where she lived,
was at the time being heavily bombed. Each night brought
its terrors; each morning its shattered streets, its smell of
rubble in the rain. None of these, however, disturbed
the habit, discipline, ingrained urge—it could be described
in many ways—which brought this woman to Communion
early each day. One morning, after a very severe night's
bombing, apart from the celebrant, she was the only
person present. 'Ye that do truly and earnestly repent
you of your sins, and are in love and charity with your
neighbours. . . .' The words seemed to carry an extra
weight of meaning that morning. And then, as the chalice
was handed to the solitary communicant, a delayed-action
bomb went off outside. The building shook; windows

shattered, glass poured in. The hands that took the chalice, however, never faltered, nor did the woman herself for the rest of the service react in any way to the rather daunting circumstances. To attempt to say why, to hazard any guess as to the source of such unassailable calm, would surely be to trespass into what the woman herself would certainly have regarded not only as private territory; but as an area of experience which she would have had no words to describe. It is possible only to record the facts, which may be regarded as remarkable or unremarkable, according to taste. There is one other fact which should perhaps be recorded—the influence of this woman's Christian witness upon some of those who noticed it. 'We never know,' wrote William Temple, 'who is doing the greatest work for God. Here is a man who holds great office in the Church, and preaches to multitudes; yet at the end all he has done is to keep things from falling back. And there is a girl, poor and uneducated, of whom no one ever thinks: but because she is loving and devout, she sows the seeds of life. . . .'

And then—the last of these memories—there was the farmer, a man whose deeply embedded faith was focused upon the Church in a particular place, and expressed through services to the local community. Continuity and locality meant very much to this man: churchwarden, parish councillor, good neighbour. For him, those feet walked upon England's mountains green, and the holy Lamb of God was still seen there to a considerable extent because they had done so for his forbears. Significantly, the church where he worshipped, not always without grumblings and sharp criticisms about what went on there, was a very ancient one. The Farmer, modern in all respects in his own business, had the utmost reverence for this antique setting, stoutly bore witness there to a Master who, it is possible to feel, liked him very much, and, in a time of bewildering social and economic change, seemed to hold the local community together, through his own integrity and sense of Christian obligation. It is much to be hoped that, after his time, there will be others like him to follow him, a consideration worth bearing in mind when we come to think about the pressures now bearing upon the fairly simple faith of such as he. A suitable epitaph for him might well be one used of a seventeenth-century countryman in Devon:

> Here lies Will Burgoin, a squire by descent
> Whose death in this world many people lament;
> The rich for his love
> The poor for his alms
> The wife for his knowledge
> The sick for his balms.
> Grace did he love and vice control
> Earth has his body, Heaven his soul.

Such then they are, or were, because people no longer with us have deliberately been chosen to provide these instances. Thus treated, they may well appear, like dried flowers, less natural than in fact they were. And certainly, no extraordinary virtues are claimed for them, nor any uniqueness. Nor is it for a moment suggested that such cover the whole spectrum of Christian character. There are many other kinds of Christians besides this particular sort. And even if they have their virtues, they certainly have their faults, of which a resistance to change is probably the chief and most injurious. The only significance in the undoubted fact that they are not so much rare as typical, lies in the evidence thus presented of their number,

But they are very important people in terms of the future of the Christian faith in this land, with all that that implies not only in personal lives, but as an influence upon the whole tone and nature of our society. They have, moreover, always been *in* our society quietly holding up, like the solid pillars of some foundation which few visit, but which is essential to the safety of the building above, the values by which the majority still live. These values in the last resort depend upon the consciousness that human life has a larger dimension than the entirely material, and that men and women can be sustained by a larger hope and are answerable to a loftier judgement than any which this world affords. The testimony to the existence of such values in the last resort is found in the lives of those who profess them. The intangible at that point becomes tangible. 'They took note of them, that they had been with Jesus' men said of the first disciples; and it is surely not too much to say that something like the same reaction is many a time unconsciously evoked by the Quiet Christians of this world. But insofar as the faith they profess is so much a matter of the unseen and intangible, and insofar as it is usually inarticulately held, it can be wilted, if too many cold winds of criticism blow upon it too often. Something like that is happening now. The immediate point, however, is the value and importance, both influential far beyond the confines of their own lives, of the witness these Quiet People have to offer.

They have had many antecedents, and it is fascinating to follow the traces of them backwards in time. What faith sustained the worthy citizen of Burford in the Cotswolds, for instance, upon whose tomb in the clock-ticking church may be read these words:

> Drive out fear from heart, O my body. I believe that you shall appear before God in Christ; for he it is that sustains you and calls you to dwell with him. Laugh at the threats of disease, despise the blows of misfortune, care not for the dark grave and go forward at Christ's summons. For Christ will be to each man a kingdom, a light, a life and a crown.

The date was 1569, a time of considerable perturbation in affairs. Ours is not the first age, after all, nor surely will it be the last, to feel itself involved in a 'shaking of the foundations.' Yet here was this Burford citizen dying, as no doubt he had lived, in a strong hope, a sure faith very characteristically resting in Christ alone, and sustaining him through all the changes and chances of a fleeting world. The very phraseology of the inscription reflects that individual religion which, developing in the late Middle Ages, was greatly strengthened by the Reformation emphasis upon the personal accountability of everyone before his God. From that source comes much of the tradition of undemonstrative Christian practice typical of those whom we have called the Quiet People.

A whole range of devotional literature came into existence, notably in the seventeenth century and onwards—it exists to this day, and is still being produced—to meet the needs of people who wished to examine their consciences, to pray, to be guided through the scriptures, to build up their spiritual lives. The thread of this literature can be traced through the tapestry of English life for the last three centuries. From the *Private Devotions* of Lancelot Andrewes, Jeremy Taylor's *Holy Living and Dying*, the anonymous *Whole Duty of Man*, William Law's *Serious Call to a Devout and Holy Life*, Wilberforce's *Practical View* to Keble's *Christian Year*, the list is a long one. The modest understatement of spiritual aspiration privately yet ardently pursued is epitomized in a well-known verse from this last:

> The trivial round, the common task
> Would furnish all we need to ask;
> Room to deny ourselves, a road
> To bring us, daily, nearer God.

So believe many of the Quiet People in any age, including this one, the meanwhile going about their business, whatever it may be, instinctively concealing any outward evidence of the fact.

These writings have not survived only on their own merits; but by the fact that they have always had enough readers—and some, such as *The Christian Year*, have been best sellers. (Just as, in far more recent times, and in another, but related, *genre* have been the writings of C. S. Lewis.) The question is: who were the readers? They can surely, by the very nature of the books them-selves, have been for the most part none other than the kind of people we are particularly thinking of here, so that this literature which has emerged, generation after generation, to meet their needs, is among the evidence of their reality and the marks of their passage.

Nor are they the only ones. There are few parishes which do not contain memories of people of this sort who have so served God in their day and generation as to have left a mark. Sometimes, if rarely, it is an actual memorial; more often a tradition of service and devotion. And sometimes it is a warm family memory of goodness, kindness and integrity. The sum total is formidable. Such people have graced our spiritual landscape for a long time as its oaks have graced the vanishing country-side. We should miss them. And always their faith has been markedly Christocentric, so that another verse in the same poem of Keble's is characteristic of it:

> Sun of my soul, thou Saviour dear
> It is not night if thou be near.
> Oh! may no earth-born cloud arise
> To hide thee from thy servant's eyes.

But several earth-born clouds have in fact arisen. And it is precisely because there are so many of them, and because so many seem to have appeared simultaneously, that one feels the need to speak now to those who are disconcerted by them. Nor must it be forgotten that these same clouds overshadow the man or woman who wants to believe but finds it hard. Portraiture is perhaps here unnecessary, because most of us can provide our own, or even find it in a mirror! They are as much daunted by the increasing secularization of the climate we all live in as are those who do believe but find it harder than it used to be.

So secularization is one cloud. Another, which is only a cloud if it is regarded as such, is formed by the atmo-sphere of the questioning of old certitudes in which all thinking Christians now have to live. This questioning is inevitable, understandable, necessary, and happening equally in other areas of inquiry, including the scientific. To imagine that the forms the Christian faith takes, the language and liturgy in which it is expressed, even the understanding of the faith itself are going to remain unaltered, or ever should remain unaltered, in an age of

such rapid change as this is to imagine a vain thing. It is
not Christians who of late have turned the world upside
down so much as the scientists and technologists, and
clearly they are going to go on doing so. How inevitable,
therefore, and how necessary as a concomitant to this
process is that radical re-thinking of Christian fundamentals
which has been going on now for a long time. Quiet People,
Christian, or would-be, must get used to coming upon
such statements as this from an article in *Time* magazine—
'It is the 20th century, the age of technological miracle,
that has seen the triumph of the Enlightenment and the
apparent banishment of God from the universe—even,
thanks to Freud, from the human soul. Writing from his
German prison cell in 1944 the anti-Nazi martyr, Dietrich
Bonhoeffer, defined it as "the world come of age", in
which "man has learned to cope with all the questions of
importance without recourse to God as a working
hypothesis. . . ." As usual, it was Bonhoeffer who best
expressed the millennial hope for the coming of God's
kingdom that lies behind the theology of renewal. "The
day will come," he wrote from his prison cell, "when men
will be called again to utter the word of God with such
power as will change and renew the world. It will be a
new language, which will horrify men, and yet over-
whelm them by its power." '

But in the meantime there can be no doubt that this
re-thinking of fundamentals can do violent things to
a faith which has become settled into its own particular
grooves. This has, of course, happened before. 'Perhaps
the more extreme Reformers were trying to do too much,'
wrote C. J. Stranks speaking in *Anglican Devotion*,[1] of the

---

[1] C. J. Stranks, *Anglican Devotion*, S.C.M.

liturgical ferment of the mid-sixteenth century, 'and so went beyond the capacity of many people. Undoubtedly they threw away a great deal that was valuable in the effort to clear the ground, but their aim at least was noble. . . .' With that we would fully concur, humbly recognizing the need of those many modern reformers who seek new insights for a new age. Perhaps it has always been a fault of the Quiet People that they have sought an abiding city while forgetting that, as the writer of Hebrews put it, 'here we have no permanent home, but we are seekers after the city which is to come.' And so they tend to have a built-in tenderness, often as extreme in the second kind of Quiet Person as in the first, to anything which seems to call in question long-established and much-loved traditions of these fields, forgetting the danger, as Latourette puts it, in *The Prospect for Christianity*, 'of insisting that the forms of Christianity which have been handed down from the past are for all times the normal and final expressions of the Gospel,' together with the equal danger of forgetting that 'As environment and cultures change, they become more and more out of touch with them, and are clung to by dwindling minorities.'[1]

But today's environment and culture will continue to change. The 'shaking of the foundations' will extend into tomorrow as well. And this process will as a certainty affect more and more cherished spiritual possessions. The successors today of the people like the Draper, the Soldier, the Housekeeper, the Farmer, must expect this to happen and strive to make themselves less vulnerable when it does. Above all, they, like all of us, need to try and see, through all the vastly changing scene, what Peter

[1] K. S. Latourette, *The Prospect for Christianity*, Eyre & Spottiswoode.

and John beheld on the Mount of Transfiguration when the tabernacles of Moses and Elijah had disappeared— Jesus only. And one of the purposes behind this little book will be, in fact, to try and do just that. Meanwhile, the broad truth remains that, insofar as any of us feel ourselves affected by what some regard as chill winds of change, it is well to remind ourselves, to draw again upon the writer of Hebrews, that we are not dwellers in any fortress of certitude. 'We look backward,' said the Dean of St. Paul's, in *Strangers and Pilgrims*, 'at the pleasant days we have known, and we linger in the past, reluctant to let it go. . . . But to the pilgrim these passages should not be wholly sad. . . . These phases of life are incidents of the journey; but it is the way that matters, not the accidents of the road. The time has come to move on? Then break up the camp with a good heart: it is only one more stage on the journey home! One day we shall break camp for the last time in this world, and face the final adventure of death. May we then have so passed the days of our pilgrimage, with the Lord of Adventurers by our side, that we may reach, in the end, our eternal home.'[1]

Meanwhile, just as in any city which has been 'developed' the tall new buildings, hard faced and impersonal, seem to overpower the older and smaller, including the churches, so in our world now the things of the spirit seem overwhelmed. What is happening is quite simple in essence, if complex in its manifestations. It is that the areas in which God for so long seemed self evidently to reign: as solace in fear, light in darkness, strength in weakness, have been progressively eroded by advancing human knowledge. This, after all, was always

[1] W. R. Matthews, *Strangers and Pilgrims*, Nisbet.

little more than a 'God of the gaps'; something or someone to whom we appealed, like primitive man on hearing
the thunder, when fear came or misfortune struck. But as
we all become self-sufficient, just by living in a world
where, more or less, man controls events, so the need for
God in this sense seems to grow less.

But the need for a God who may be personally encountered, whom we can know and who we can feel
knows us, does not grow less. On the contrary, it grows
more acute as our world becomes increasingly impersonal.
'The experience and the claim of Christians have always
been that it is in the life and person and teaching of Christ
that God is most clearly shown,' writes Professor Rhodes
in his essay *Christianity in a Mechanistic Universe*. 'In the
historical person of Christ, God may be known. It is, in
fact, at this point, in him, that science and faith meet. . . .
The scientific method of observation and analysis would
be an inadequate way of becoming familiar with a new
next-door neighbour. . . . To do so I must myself participate in the encounter as a person. So also if there is any
possibility that the Christian claim of a personal God may
be true, the detached scientific approach must be utterly
inadequate to make his acquaintance. I must participate
as a person in whatever encounters there may be with him.'

And so also we may say that the possibility of encounter
with this personal Christ, who down the centuries has
marvellously made himself known to men and women,
is that which, we believe, beyond all else now can bring
reassurance to those many who are feeling it hard either
to persist in or to discover a living faith. And so it is that
encounter, the form which it has taken, and the consequences which have flowed from it at different times, and
in different lives, which will here be our concern.

2. The Heart of the Matter

AT THE heart of all Christian experience, then, is an encounter with Jesus Christ, This encounter can take many shapes, far more than is always recognized. One of the several sad consequences of the separation of the sacred from the secular—of the notion that there is something called 'religion' and something called 'life' and that never the twain shall meet—has been limitation of what might be called, for want of a better term, religious experience to the field of pietistic experience. Just as the events of Pentecost have come to be regarded by many as somehow representing the sum-total of the activities of the Holy Spirit, so the possibility of the Christ encounter has been seen in similarly limited terms, as something necessarily confined to certain specialized areas of experience; prayer, worship, devotion and the like. But this is not so. As the activity of the Holy Spirit, dynamic and creative from age to age, is to be found as much in great art and science as in what have come to be regarded as more specifically 'religious' activities, so Christ can be met with surely in more situations than is commonly supposed. 'Lord, when was it that we saw you hungry and fed you, or thirsty and gave you drink, a stranger and took you home, or naked and clothed you?' ask the righteous in the vision of Judgement in Matthew 25, genuinely surprised at being numbered among the elect. So is it still with many who, willing in the service of their fellow men and women, remain unaware that in so doing they are meeting Christ whenever there is human need to be met and compassion shown. And even this is only one of the bewilderingly many directions from which he comes towards us. He can come as well as through beauty, joy, high endeavour for a good purpose, also through suffering, and be found as a light in many a dark place of the soul. 'Come to me, all whose work is hard, whose load is heavy: and I will give you relief.' There is nothing exclusive about that 'all,' and the notion that anyone has to pass some kind of spiritual means test in order to come within the scope of the promise has no warrant in scripture. There must therefore be many who have encountered Christ without recognizing him. Like the two on the road to Emmaus 'something held their eyes from seeing who it was' when Jesus 'came up and walked along with them.' The world of men is not, in fact, nearly as empty of Christ as some suppose, nor encounters with him as rare and specialized as many think.

Even so, there are three classic forms of Christ encounter which we propose to look at here: the gospel account of the gradual transformation of the character of the Galilean fisherman, Simon, through contact with the Christ, into a personality infinitely greater; some instances of Christ encounter through mystical experience, and some cases of confrontations with him in the highways and byways of ordinary life which, as we have said, happen more often than many suppose.

There have been several writers who have delighted to see in Simon an instance of the 'ordinary man' whose great potentialities for heroism, faith and service were realized through the service of Christ. Similarly Studdert Kennedy, writing years ago of his experiences during the first world war, recalled how, finding a dead soldier, with the name Peter in his pay-book, was instantly put in mind of his Galilean namesake, and of how his life was transformed in a manner which, he felt sorrowfully sure, had not come the way of the dead soldier because the Church had failed to tell him of Christ in sufficiently challenging terms. All such treatments of New Testament narratives and figures incur obvious dangers, not the least of them that of reading the gospels in an ingenuous way, and of forcing contemporary interpretations into a mould never designed to take them. Yet the gospels abound in living portraits of people who encountered Christ face to face. The significance of their reactions as to the deep and subtle nature of that encounter may have to be dug for further beneath the surface than was once supposed, just as the gospels themselves are now seen to be far more complex documents, both as regards structure and intention, than was once thought. But the clues are there, nonetheless; particularly so in the case of Simon Peter. What is the clue to the nature of the Christ encounter embedded in, for instance, the outwardly simple tale of 'the miraculous draught of fishes'?[1] What is the writer saying to us through the puzzling reaction of Simon who, realizing it was the Christ who was in the boat with him, instead of rejoicing at the catch of fish, experienced instead a sharp sense of personal unworthiness? 'Go, Lord, leave me, sinner that I am' he cries.

Let's look at this more closely. One morning, after a night's fishing during which Simon had caught nothing, when he was washing his nets, he saw a crowd on the shore. Jesus, the carpenter from Nazareth, was there. The crowd showed how his fame had begun to spread. Then the fisherman heard his name called. 'Simon, I

[1] Luke 5. 3–11.

would like to use your boat.' So Jesus entered, and standing in the stern, began to speak. When he had finished, he turned to Simon. 'Put out into deep water and let down your nets for a catch.' Simon, as a fisherman, would have known the improbability of catching fish by day when it had already proved impossible by night. And so he voiced his doubts. 'Master, we were hard at work all night and caught nothing at all.' Jesus looked at him—one of those glances mentioned several times in the gospels. Simon began to realize that he might have been mistaken, and so added the significant line: 'but if you say so, I will let down the nets.' And so he did so, and this time the net came up so full of fish that Simon had to ask help from his partners in a boat nearby to help haul in. Both boats, before they were through, were over-loaded. The narrative, behind its outward simplicities, is mysterious. Like the boats after the catch, it is heavy to the gunwales with significance. Why is Peter so prominent? And is there not here implicit a reminder to the Church of Luke's own time—or of any other time, including our own—that those who obey the call of the Lord to fish faithfully, in the true sense of that word, in the waters of the world for the souls of men, will assuredly bring them in? But what has it to tell also of the Christ encounter as it affects the personality involved? That is the matter with which we are here principally concerned. Here again there is abundance. Simon begins with doubt, as many a man has done. Christ comes into his life apparently by chance, while he is busy with other things, as Simon was with his fishing when Jesus appeared on the shore. Then he is drawn to do something for him, as Simon allowed him the use of his boat. Then he hears a command of the Lord, but sees little sense in it, in

comparison with what he, as a practical man, knows, or
thinks he knows, of the realities of the situation. Yet he
obeys, because he respects the commander. Here, surely,
is an essential first step towards Christ commitment, a
movement uncertain as a child's initial attempt at walking, and equally as likely to be followed by a fall, but yet a
first step—an act of will and obedience, of experimental
trust qualified by many inner doubts. Simon's words, as
the New English Bible has them, come alive here. He
sees little sense in fishing again where before he had
failed. But he says to Jesus, '*if you say so*, I will.'

The story gives the sequel. But why is it followed by the
impulsive outburst of 'Go, Lord, leave me, sinner
that I am!' Here, surely, is being shown to us a second
stage in the Christ encounter—an experience which can
be so highly disturbing, because it reveals us to ourselves
as we really are, that some have wished it had never come
upon them. It has been well said that the arch-deceiver
in any man's life is himself. We hide from ourselves what
we really are. But contact with the truth of Christ makes
that impossible, for he it is 'unto whom all hearts are
open, all desires known, and from whom no secrets are
hid.' In his presence we see, as many have found, the
truth about ourselves, and it is often disturbing, like the
discovery of unsuspected physical dirt revealed by un-
familiar surgical standards of cleanliness. The gospel
narrative, in featuring this odd reaction of Simon's in
the boat, is therefore telling us more than that it was,
as one commentary puts it, 'a recognition of the supernatural in Jesus,' whatever that may mean. It is telling us
that a further stage in the Christ encounter is this sudden,
extremely startling realization of his holiness and power,
and of our own unworthiness to be in such company at all,

because of what we know about ourselves, even if no one else does.

This is crucial. So long as we are satisfied with ourselves, we are not likely ever to be repentant for what we are. And so long as we cannot repent, so long, equally, can we not know what forgiveness means, nor experience the joy of acceptance arising from the humble realization that, if strict divine justice were to be done, we should be rejected. The joy in heaven over one sinner who repents has meaning here, for repentance is a step towards the truth in Christ, and towards fuller life in his service. Meanwhile, self-sufficiency and self-satisfaction, the characteristic mental postures of our own day and age, surely do more than any number of imaginary sins to keep us, materially comfortable as we are, from a realization of the truth that we can do 'nothing of ourselves to help ourselves' as the Prayer Book quaintly puts it. But the 'Go, Lord, leave me, sinner that I am' of Simon in the boat is now, as it was then, strangely enough, more a movement towards Christ than away from him.

Yet Simon had still to recognize in his own mind, in the very centre of his own personality, who this Jesus was in the whole scheme of things. The realization came at Caesarea Philippi, where Jesus put to his followers the question which lies now as then at the source of all faith in him. The importance of the happenings at Caesarea Philippi[1] cover, of course, an immense field. But in the matter of the individual encounter with Christ they are also crucial. What was involved was a further act of will. Self-surrender was the first. Here now was the second— intellectual acceptance of Christ, without reservations.

[1] Matthew 16. 13–20.

'Who do men say that the Son of Man is?' This is the question. They gave him the answer to be expected from men familiar with the tradition that the mighty dead would appear as heralds of the Messianic age. That the Messiah himself stood before them was to be realized by only one of them. And so they said: 'Some say John the Baptist, others Elijah, others Jeremiah, or one of the prophets.' The Lord turned to Simon. 'Who do you say I am?' So they paused. Simon alone, his mind filled with a great truth, got the right answer: 'I believe that you are the Christ, the son of the living God.' His will had been brought to the point of obedience many months before. But only now was his mind convinced of the essential fact about Christ—his divinity and uniqueness. Thus the shape of the Christ encounter of Simon Peter begins to emerge. It begins with an act of minor obedience hedged around with many private reservations, passing very soon afterwards, through a startled realization of something transcendent and mysterious in the Christ, to a sharp sense of personal unworthiness. This in its turn leads to deeper commitment. Fuller understanding follows, and at Caesarea Philippi the truth about this Jesus, first met as a man among men, the carpenter's son from Nazareth, is revealed.

And there, in an ideal world, the story would end. But this world is far from ideal: in any age it is violent and tragic, and the affairs of men in it are marked indelibly by that flaw in human nature which, unredeemed, is fatal. So Simon Peter, having thus encountered the Lord, should have served him to that glorious consummation of his ministry which Peter, with the rest of the disciples, assumed would follow when they went finally up to Jerusalem. Yet in fact what happened was a betrayal—

a sombre warning that even the apparently complete Christian commitment can fade away if it is not, if need be, prepared to go to the Cross itself. The story as Luke has it is told with a poignant vividness probably derived from Peter's own account of the night's happenings when Jesus was captured by the servants of the High Priest and taken bound into the palace. Simon followed at a distance. Cold and heart-sick he tried to warm himself in front of a brazier. At this point a serving-maid looked across the firelight at him, saying; ' "This man was with him, too." But he denied it. "Woman," he said, "I do not know him!" A little later someone else noticed him, and said: "You are also one of them." But Peter said to him, "No, I am not." About an hour passed and another spoke more strongly still: "Of course this fellow was with him. He must have been; he is a Galilean." But Peter said, "Man, I do not know what you are talking about!" At that moment, while he was still speaking, a cock crew: and the Lord turned and looked straight at Peter.'[1]

Yet the end was triumph after all; but it was a triumph which arose, in the cycle of Christian experience, through death and resurrection. The Peter of history, the rock-man, the kind of person upon whom the Church could be built, had to encounter the risen Christ before his own commitment could become so total as to be beyond reach of fear, or doubt, or further betrayal. The story ends, where it began, by the lakeside. The narrative, possibly from another writer than that of the main body of the Fourth Gospel, and certainly written long after the events it describes, is mysterious. The disciples have fished all night, and caught nothing. And then there is Christ on

[1] Luke 22. 56-61.

the shore in the early light speaking, telling them to cast again, which they do, and catch many. The writer completes the tale.

'When they came ashore, they saw a charcoal fire there, with fish laid on it, and some bread. Jesus said, "Bring some of your catch." Simon Peter went aboard and dragged the net to land, full of big fish, a hundred and fifty-three of them; and yet, many as they were, the net was not torn. Jesus said, "Come and have breakfast." None of the disciples dared to ask "Who are you?" '[1] They knew it was the Lord, just as Christians have met him in the Eucharist from age to age. Jesus now came up, took the bread, and gave it to them, and the fish in the same way.

'After breakfast, Jesus said to Simon Peter, "Simon, son of John, do you love me more than all else?" "Yes, Lord," he answered, "you know that I love you." "Then feed my lambs" he said. A second time he asked, "Simon son of John, do you love me?" "Yes, Lord, you know I love you." "Then tend my sheep." A third time he said, "Simon son of John, do you love me?" Peter was hurt that he asked him a third time, "Do you love me?" "Lord," he said, "you know everything; you know I love you." Jesus said, "Feed my sheep."

' "And further, I tell you this in very truth: when you were young you fastened your belt about you and walked where you chose; but when you are old you will stretch out your arms, and a stranger will bind you fast, and carry you where you have no wish to go." He said this to indicate the manner of death by which Peter was to glorify God. Then he added, "Follow me." '[2]

[1] John 21. 9-12. [2] John 21. 15-19.

'Follow me —.' That is necessarily and always the result of the Christ encounter. It is, indeed, the infallible test of its reality, and an essential part of the obedience involved is a willingness to be led without knowing the course of the journey, without expecting it to be easy, and with a clear realization that, if Christian history and experience be any guide, the earthly end might be desolation. Peter's martyrdom was indicated in the very passage in which his call to supreme discipleship was made plain. Those who speak too easily of the Christ encounter should pause at this point. Discipleship is either costly or it is nothing. Its reality depends upon the degree to which its consequences are felt in the daily traffic of the world; in the home, at work, in all personal relationships, in all attitudes to life, in the uses of our energies, goods, and time. Lacking that, it is either words or emotion only. That it is 'a fearful thing to fall into the hands of the living God' can be true of this encounter, as well. Herein lies its challenge: a challenge to courage, faith and fortitude. Its joy lies in the companionship of him who comes to us still, as he came to Simon Peter, by the lakesides of life, when we are busy with other matters, and says 'follow me.'

. . . . .

'For those fortunate enough to see and know God in the person of Jesus Christ, the human being,' wrote J. B. Phillips in *New Testament Christianity*, 'and recognize who he was, the faculty of faith was naturally stimulated and confirmed. Peter, for example, blurts out a truth which others beside himself must have been thinking when he exclaims: "Thou hast the words of eternal life . . ." In this exclamation, and in "Thou art the Christ, the Son of

B

the Living God," Peter is saying that the very focal-point
of faith is alive before them, the heart and centre of the
unseen eternal dimension has broken into the time and
space set-up in visible form.'[1]

He goes on to say how easy it is to think how slow were
those who encountered Christ in the flesh to see beyond
the humanity to the divinity. Yet it is a tardiness to which
men in all ages have been prone. We are slow ourselves
to make this act of recognition when we encounter him
in some of the many ways in which he comes to us now
in the highways and byways of life. It is important here
to check with ourselves as to whether really, in our heart
of hearts, we *expect* to meet him. If we do not live with this
expectation we shall not merely be slow to know him when
he comes: we shall be blind to the vision of him even
when he stands beside us. And what chiefly keeps us blind
in this way is the absence of that quality of life which, for
want of a better word, we may call 'faith.' Phillips is
helpful upon this point also: 'It is a pity that we have to
use the word "faith" to describe the faculty by which
the unseen dimension is grasped, drawn upon, and lived
by . . . Suppose it is true as I am sure it is, that we are
at all times surrounded and permeated by this spiritual
dimension. Suppose, too, that we needed the X-faculty
in order to appreciate this further dimension. Can we not
see that it is the X-faculty which has deteriorated over
the centuries between us and the Church's young days?
I believe we all have this faculty, but in many of us it has
become atrophied almost to vanishing point.'[2]

But among the mystics this is not so. There, down the
generations, are to be found evidences of a continual

[1] J. B. Phillips, *New Testament Christianity*, Hodder & Stoughton.
[2] Ibid.

penetration of this spiritual dimension, and of encounters with the living Christ therein. In an age as materialist as ours, when there is so much to shut us off from the world of the spirit, including currently fashionable denials of its existence, to turn to the testimony of such is to be refreshed indeed. An important part, therefore, of the proclaiming of Christ today, and of the continued possibility of encounter with him, is to take note of the manners in which these people have from age to age walked with him.

It is natural to turn to St. Francis to begin with— natural because of all the saints and of all the mystics he is the one who seems most to speak to the condition of everyman, perhaps because he met with Christ so clearly among the familiar scenes of everyday. So Assisi might be anybody's town, glorified by having the light of heaven shining upon it. And the young Francis, before he met with the Lord, might be any gay young man with his life before him, living well in a rather mindless good time society. The reason why his story appeals so widely lies surely in the fact that in it so many have seen the realization of a wistful dream of their own, that they too may meet with Christ, and have the best within them drawn out by that encounter.

The tale has often enough been told of how the high-spirited youth, comfortably off as the son of a rich merchant, after a spell of military service, became disenchanted with the ways of the world as he knew them. So he turned to prayer and the service of the poor. But soon he was more deeply committed. On a pilgrimage to Rome the spectacle of the teeming beggars outside St. Peter's moved him, characteristically impulsive, to take the rags of one, and beg himself. Henceforth he was vowed to poverty. The world thought him mad: his father disowned him. But the lepers around Assisi, those untouchables of the middle ages, came to know and love him as he devoted himself to their service. There was a ruined church nearby, St. Damiano's. As one day he knelt before the altar, the Lord, as legend has it, called him by name: 'Francis, go and repair my house which, as thou seest, is in ruins.' And then, in the Church of the Portiuncula—Santa Maria Degli Angeli, he received his 'call.' It came through a hearing of that passage in Matthew,[1] where the Lord commissions the disciples, bidding them, as part of the preaching of the Kingdom, to abandon material possessions. The moment and the place became the points of origin of one of the most fruitful of Christian enterprises, the Franciscan Order, which took Christ's love into the stinking alleys of mediaeval Europe as nothing else did, relieving the brutality and sordidness of the times. Sixteen years later, ill, worn-out, yet strangely happy, Francis, in retreat on Mount Alvernia in the Appenines, received, it is told, the Stigmata. Two years later he was dead. But before the end he had written a hymn of praise which bears quoting and needs remembering in times of spiritual drought such as ours. This man, truly, had met with the Lord. His life bears unshakeable witness to the reality of it.

> All holy art Thou, Lord God, God of Gods;
> Sole maker of all miracles; strong and great!
> The highest art Thou and Omnipotent;
> Thou art the Father, King of Heaven and Earth,
> Trinity and Unity, Lord, and God of Gods.
> Thou art the perfect good—sole highest good—
> The true and only Lord, the living God.
> And Thou art Charity, Wisdom, Patience, Joy,

[1] Matthew 10. 7-19.

Security, Beauty, Justice, Quietude . . .
Thou art Humility, and Thou art our Hope,
Our Temperance, and our Peace, our Fortitude.
Thou art the only riches that we need,
Our discipline, protection and our guard,
Our refuge, and our sure defence and strength.
Thou art our Faith and Hope and Charity.
Thou art our spring of sweetness welling up—
Thou mighty source of goodness infinite.
Omnipotent Lord God, mysterious, high,
Loving and merciful, our dear Saviour—Christ!

And so one could go on, dipping at random into this rich store of evidence of the recurring miracle of the Christ encounter. There is the case, for instance, of the French soldier, Charles de Foucard. Endowed, like Francis, with every worldly gift, he decided to leave the world. For ten years he led in Palestine a life of silence and prayer. Then in 1901, at the age of 42, he moved to the Sahara where he established a mission station which was to be his home till his death in 1916, experiencing continual privations, disappointments, ill health, yet being constantly renewed by the experience of Christ's presence. He wrote: 'Every day more and more I experience the certainty that I am where God wishes me to be. We must be happy, for however sad I am, when I kneel down in front of the altar and I say to our Lord, "Lord, your are infinitely happy, you lack nothing," then I cannot help adding "then I, too, am happy and I lack nothing. Your happiness suffices me".' Many years later he wrote to one of his intimate friends 'of the immense happiness which one enjoys at the thought that God is God and that He whom we love with our whole being is infinitely and eternally blessed.'

And then again Theresa of Avila: 'If, while Jesus lived in the world, the mere touch of his garments healed the sick, who can doubt that when he is dwelling in the very centre of our being he will work miracles on us if we have a living faith in him? And will he not grant our petitions while he is our guest? . . . Take pleasure in remaining in his society: do not lose such precious time, for this hour is of the utmost value to the soul, and the good Jesus desires you to spend it with him.'

And here, speaking out of another background altogether, is Hannah Whitall Smith, the Quaker. 'The heights of Christian perfection can only be reached by each moment faithfully following the guide who is to lead you there; and he reveals the way to us one step at a time, in the little things of our daily lives, asking only on our part that we yield ourselves up to his guidance— be perfectly pliable in his hands, to go where he entices you and to turn away from all which makes you shrink. Obey him perfectly the moment you are sure of his will, and you will soon find that he is leading you out swiftly and easily into such a wonderful life of conformity to himself that will be a testimony to all around you, beyond what you yourself will ever know.'

And here is William Law, most temperate and lucid of mystics: 'Poor sinner! consider the treasure thou hast within thee; the Saviour of the world, the eternal word of God lies hid in thee, as a spark of the divine nature which is to overcome sin and death and hell within thee, and generate the life of Heaven again in thy soul. Turn to thy heart and thy heart will find the Saviour, its God within itself. . . . Seek for him in thy heart and thou wilt never seek in vain, for there he dwells and there is the seat of his light and Holy Spirit . . . for though God is everywhere present, yet he is only present to thee in the deepest and most central part of thy soul.'

The painter, Van Gogh, comes to the same point by another route, a reminder that there are indeed many ways to the living God. He writes, in a letter to a friend: 'I always think that the best way to know God is to love many things. Love a friend, a wife, something—whatever you like—you will be on the way to knowing more about him. . . . But one must love with a lofty and serious intimate sympathy, with strength, with intelligence; and one must always try to know deeper, better, and more. That leads to God, that leads to unwavering faith. . . .'

He goes on to speak, as many have done, of the liberating power of love, setting the soul free from the self-made prisons which keep so many constricted souls from contact with Christ. 'Do you know what frees one from this captivity? It is every deep, serious affection. Being friends, being brothers, *love*, that is what opens the prison by some supreme power, by some magic force— without this one remains in prison—where sympathy is renewed, life is restored.'

Such a passage—and indeed such a writer—clearly stands apart from the classic tradition of spiritual autobiography. We have here a different kind of person, speaking out of a tradition entirely different from that of a Francis, or a Theresa of Avila, or a de Foucard; speaking, indeed out of no particular tradition at all. The point is well made in Anne Freemantle's most valuable book, *The Protestant Mystics*, from which some of these illustrations are drawn. Catholic mysticism, she suggests, has tended to follow a relatively narrow path, marked out by usage and

[1] Anne Freemantle, *The Protestant Mystics*, Weidenfeld & Nicolson.

tradition: protestant mysticism, on the other hand, has often tended more to spill over into the secular world, and to find its starting point therein. Sometimes less intense, because more diffuse, it has nonetheless reclaimed for the sacred whole areas of the supposedly secular. Thus Van Gogh can use such terms as 'supreme power,' and 'magic force' in the context in the deepening of human relationships—'being friends, being brothers'—which love brings. Such a passage may well be compared with Father Zossima in Dostoevsky's *The Brothers Karamazov*: 'Love all God's creation, both the whole, and every grain of sand. Love every leaf, every ray of light, love the animals, love the plants, love each separate thing. If thou love each thing then thou wilt perceive the mystery of God in all. . . .'

'In all'—those are surely the key words to an understanding of the fact that we have, many of us, quite needlessly limited the areas in which we *expect* to encounter God. One of the gravest consequences of this shrinkage is that a faith which has always claimed all the world of human experience for its own is seen as something far more limited than is in fact the case.

The point is of some importance to this matter of the Christ encounter which we are here discussing. Is it possible, for instance, that we have come nowadays so to limit the area of our expectations of such an encounter, and so to formalize the terms of it, as to have become blind to the possibilities of meeting him in other places and in other contexts. Many people, for instance, to look at one very important possibility, have known moments of strange exaltation arising from contact with the beauties of the natural world. What is this: pantheism only—the hearing of that pagan god stamping his

foot in a thicket, as Stevenson put it? W. H. Auden, in
his introduction to Miss Freemantle's book, would appear
to suggest so. Speaking of this kind of mystical experience,
he says, 'The basic experience is an overwhelming conviction that the objects confronting him had a numinous
significance and importance, that the existence of everything he is aware of is holy. And the basic emotion is one
of innocent joy, though this joy can include, of course, a
reverent dread.' But why should such an experience be
categorized as necessarily non-Christian? The point is
touched upon in the next two sections of this book where
the writers, working quite independently of each other,
both find it necessary, when trying to outline something
of their own spiritual experiences, to attach considerable
importance to experiences of this very sort.

Meanwhile, it is significant that Miss Freemantle in her
book, sees fit to include a passage from that determined
atheist Richard Jefferies. Yet who, reading this extract
from *The Story of My Heart*, cannot applaud her judgement, sense the strong spiritual and moral element in the
writing, catching it in echoes of experiences of his own
and, if a Christian, feel eager to claim that the glory
encountered in such moments shines from the Lord
himself?

'There was a time when a weary restlessness came upon
me, perhaps from too-long-continued labour. It was like
a drought—a moral drought—as if I had been absent for
many years from the sources of life and hope . . . some
instinctive feeling uncontrollably drove me to the sea. . . .
I stood where the foam came to my feet, and looked over
the sunlit waters. The great earth bearing the richness
of the harvest was at my back, its strength and firmness
under me, the great sun shone above, the wide sea was
B*

before me, the wind came sweet and strong from the waves. The life of the earth and the sea, the glow of the sun filled me; I touched the surge with my hand, I lifted my face to the sun, I opened my lips to the wind. I prayed aloud in the roar of the waves . . . "give me fullness of life like to the sea and the sun, to the earth and the air; give me fullness of physical life, mind equal and beyond their fullness; give me a greatness and perfection of soul higher than all things" . . . The earth and sun were to me like my flesh and blood and the air of the sea, life . . . Once more I touched the sea and sand farewell. So deep was the inhalation of this life that day that it seemed to remain in me for years—this was a real pilgrimage.'

All these, in their different ways, are, in the exact sense of the word, extraordinary people, with a capacity for spiritual response of a similar order. What, however, are the possibilities of Christ encounter in the lives of ordinary people, and what forms is it likely to take? There are perhaps two ways of answering this. The first is to draw upon the testimonies of others, and to report at second hand what has happened to this or that person down the corridors of time who have, as they believe, met with him and been changed by the experience. Such an undertaking would not be difficult, for there are many of them. The second way of trying to answer the question—to attempt to set down what has happened to oneself in this regard—is, however, much more difficult because fraught with so many dangers of self-deception on the one hand, and misunderstanding on the other. It is, even so, a method which the writers of this little book, very conscious of being ordinary people themselves, propose now, for the sake of the record, to venture upon.

3. *This Happened to Me*

WILLIAM PURCELL

IT IS possible to sympathize with the Bishop who once told John Wesley that the claiming of special gifts of the Holy Spirit was a very horrid thing. One sees what he was getting at. To make any personalized assertion of traffic with the divine is to incur various dangers, of which the possibility of being thought a spiritual exhibitionist is the least. Far greater is the peril of seeming to make the whole thing easier than is in fact the case, and the claims behind it—that this or that individual has had a personal, life-changing encounter with God—seem less extraordinary than indeed it is. Both devalue the experience. It may be possible to know God: it should never be possible to assume an undue familiarity. To say, therefore, that, so far as one can honestly ascertain, Christ has entered into one's life, is to make a statement which needs the most careful evaluation.

So far as this present writer is concerned no claim whatever to any dramatic, instantly recognizable moment of encounter can be made. To say that is to place oneself with the majority. Those who have been fortunate enough to experience their own Damascus road, when they knew suddenly a light from heaven and that the light was Jesus, have always been few.

It may well be necessary, as Nicodemus was told, to be born again. But the process can be slow indeed, and often requires, as with physical birth, a long period of gestation

following some secret and unknown moment of conception. It might even be said that with many people
re-birth scarcely recognizably arrives in this world at all.
Such a muted form of Christ encounter; modest, hesitant,
even doubting, may well seem considerably less impressive
than instant conversion. But the wind of the spirit blows
where it wills, so that the person concerned does not
necessarily know where it comes from or where it is going.
All he does know is that the wind has blown, and blown
his way. He knows the sound of it, and he comes to see
what it does in bending him in a direction often opposed
to that in which his background and predilections would
otherwise have moulded him. But it often has to flow a
long time before that happens. All this present writer,
therefore, is prepared to claim, is that he believes that
for him the wind of the Spirit has blown, and that with
the passage of the years he has come to have some idea of
what it has done to him. The purpose of this chapter is to
try and tell something of how it came to pass.

·   ·   ·   ·   ·

To have grown up in Britain in the twenties and thirties
is to have spent one's formative years in a long period of
disillusion. The twenties saw the beginning of that
economic blizzard which moaned dismally over public
affairs. for a very long time. The best men were dead.
Their pygmy successors struggled, for the most part
inadequately, with problems of growing intractibility,
until eventually the storm of a second world war broke.
And if the twenties were a sour time, deeply infected
by the spiritual poisons of the first war, the thirties were
the locust years in which repeated chances of avoiding a
second were thrown away. Worst of all, it was a time in

which scarcely any good cause to which youth and idealism
could give itself ever seemed to have even a modest
success. The unemployed stayed unemployed; the League
of Nations failed; the wrong side won the Spanish Civil
War. Only the appalling dictators appeared to flourish.
And when youth itself tried in those years to make a way
in the world even that modest undertaking proved
unexpectedly difficult. 'How shall a young man cleanse
his way?' asked the Psalmist. The question has rarely
been more difficult to answer than it was in the thirties.

It seems necessary to mention this matter of the background of the times in order to offer some explanation of
the fact that the atmosphere in which I grew up was
almost totally irreligious. It was not so much that my
parents had consciously rejected the Christian faith in
which they had been nurtured, as that they had allowed
it to fade quite away from among the meaningful concerns
of life. It is true that, some years before his end, my father
returned to the Church. 'Deeply spiritually minded'
an obituary notice in the parish magazine described him
at his death in 1945. 'He loved his church, and however
difficult it was for him to attend he came as regularly as
he could possibly manage. It will be strange to look
towards his seat in the north transept and find it vacant.'
My mother, too, was confirmed in the same church in her
fifties. But many things had happened by then to change
the atmosphere. It remains true that only the vestiges of
Christian commitment remained in the family life I knew
in the twenties and thirties. I remember some visits to
church. I remember the deep kindness of the Vicar of
one of them during a long absence of my father abroad
in the early twenties. Every week for more than a year
this shy man would call. I can see him now, arriving

on his bicycle, and then coming in, to look mildly upon
us, the while holding a black hat on his knee. Years later,
I think I came to understand the reasons for his love and
care. At the time it seemed incomprehensible. And that
was, and remained for a number of years, the sole contact
any of us had with the Church.

The sociology of religion has come of recent times to be
much better understood than was once the case. We know
now that the responses which people make, or fail to make,
to a given spiritual stimulus, are often greatly affected by
the political and cultural atmosphere in which they live.
And so in the twenties and thirties, when the mould of
an old world was seen to be cracked beyond repair, old
habits disappeared—and old faiths with them. It was a
bad time for the Church. More importantly, it was a
bad time for God. Periods of cynicism and disillusion
generally are. The causes which tended to attract the
enthusiasms of eager youth in the thirties were largely
political, matters of social justice above all. And it usually
seemed, however unjustly, that the Church of the day
had remarkably little to do with them. It was therefore
a natural consequence of growing up in such a time to
become totally secularized. So I had no points of contact
with spiritual things from my late adolescence almost
until my mid-twenties. 'I had a variety of concerns and
exercises about my soul from childhood,' wrote the
eighteenth-century American Calvinist Jonathan Edwards
in his *Conversion*, *Experiences and Religious Exercises*,
'but had two more remarkable seasons of awakening
before I met with that change by which I was brought
to these new dispositions.' It seems to me now that I
could make, surprisingly enough, a similar claim. There
were the 'concerns and exercises' of childhood. And later

there were several 'remarkable seasons of awakening.' Between the two there was a period of total secularization. In all, I can clearly discern six stages, six moments of truth, by which, over a period of thirty years, I believe that the Lord sought me out. In the first two of these he came to me with his face hidden, so that I knew not who or what it was who brought me that experience which Wesley once described as 'a heart strangely warmed.' I would not know now unless he had seen fit to identify himself so unmistakably in the last four of these moments of truth.

I must go back to boyhood for the first. It was upon a hillside among the Black Mountains in Wales that there came to me one of those brightly coloured fragments of time in which the level of consciousness seems sharply increased, so that all outward phenomena—sounds, colours, movements—are perceived with preternatural clarity, as though illuminated by an inner light which at the same time seems to invest them with an eternal significance. The ordinary at such time becomes extraordinary: a hillside, a drifting cloud, the movement of grass, the chuckle of a stream, all seem to have something to say, and that of which they speak seems to belong to the holy even more than to the beautiful. They speak— or these things at any rate then spoke to me—of a presence in all and through all of which two very important observations could be made: the first, that this presence deliberately, for his own good reasons, made himself to that extent known to the boy alone upon the hillside: the second, that this presence was of the very essence of all that we can mean and experience of truth and goodness. The magic of that moment has not dimmed in forty years, and the objective reality of it has stoutly survived the many attempts to explain it away in the light of adult knowledge. Such an experience could, for instance, be ascribed to the euphoria of adolescence. It could be written off as entirely subjective. It could be identified as a very common form of youthful pantheism. But other voices must also be allowed to speak. Henry Vaughan, looking back to childhood, recalls how he:

> Could see a glimpse of his bright face;
> When on some gilded cloud or flower
> My gazing soul would dwell an hour,
> And in those weaker glories spy
> Some shadows of eternity.

Such generalized intimations of something above and beyond the usual horizons of life are a long way, it is true, from a personalized encounter with Christ. But they can be a preliminary. Nor, surely, need that be thought of as odd. If the first four verses of St. John's gospel express a truth about the cosmic nature of this Christ it need surely be no cause for surprise that he should speak sometimes through the phenomena of a world which is his. 'The Word, then, was with God at the beginning, and through him all things came to be; no single thing was created without him.'

But such bright times are brief, and soon fade into the light of common day. It was so with me, except that the light was much overcast and the day very common. My years of growing up were neither happy nor profitable. When I went down from the mountain all those years ago it was in a very real sense into a valley of the shadow. The stresses of adolescence should not be under-estimated. When they are combined with an almost total lack of direction or supervision and when, moreover, they have to be endured in a world so manifestly out of joint as that of the late twenties of this century, when so many doors of opportunity seemed closed, they can be severe indeed. It followed that the next moment of truth, of a spiritual nature which came to me was of an entirely different kind. The first had been compounded of joy: this was more of desolation.

I had by that time—this would be some four wasted years after that experience on the mountain—gone off to my first job. I was alone in London, working in an advertising agency. The life was ordinary. It could even have been called satisfactory but for the discovery that it was meaningless, at any rate as I was living it. To dwell in what T. S. Eliot called the waste land, with its characteristic memorials of 'the asphalt road and a thousand lost golf balls' can be quite agreeable until the fact is recognized. Then it becomes desolating, and that I believe is what happened to me.

Suddenly, one lunch-hour, when the pigeons were feeding in the sun in Lincoln's Inn, at a spot I can identify to this day, there came upon me, with a genuine shock, the realization that if no motive or higher purpose or aim could be discovered in life beyond the mere persistence in it, then the game was simply not worth the candle. I cannot now recall whether there was any particular incident which triggered off this explosion of thought. It could possibly have been that the essential triviality of the business I was engaged—the selling of this, the writing copy for that—had that day been unusually evident. It could be that the prospect of continuing in it down the years had for the first time been examined and found daunting. Any of these things might have been the cause. But it was the result which counted. All human life, it

seemed in that moment of desolation, all the energies and
efforts, all the getting and spending, all the living and
loving, all the hoping and yearning associated with it
added up to a hollow charade—truly a tale told by an
idiot—unless at the heart of it all there was to be found
a solid core of meaning. But where was that meaning
to be found? I did not know. I knew only that I had in
that city-worker's lunch-hour become dissatisfied with
myself and the life I was living. I think that, from then
onwards, I was a man looking for something better.
But I did realize that an event of importance to my whole
inner life had transpired before I returned to my office
that day; but how important I was not to understand
until two passages come upon in the reading of later years
shed some light upon the matter. The first was in a book
called *The Healing Cross* by H. H. Farmer: 'Nothing is so
paralysing to the human spirit as the thought of ultimate
waste. Yet that is just the appearance which much in
human life seems inevitably to take on. And the more a
man loves and seeks higher things the more likely is the
grim spectre of such a thought to peer grinningly into
the face, and freeze the very marrow of the soul. What if
things are after all exactly as they seem so often to be,
and there is at the heart of the universe only a great
hole. . . .'[1]

The relevance of that to the experience in Lincoln's Inn
was at once apparent. We have often to realize what life
is without Christ before we can hope to be brought to see
the mercy of it with him.

The second passage was come upon in James's *Varieties of
Religious Experience*. An essential element in any such, he

[1] Quoted by John Baillie in *A Diary of Readings*, O.U.P., pp. 170–2.

said, consisted in 'a sense of uneasiness, a sense that something is wrong about us as we naturally stand, and a sense that we are saved from this wrongness by making proper connection with the higher powers.' Here again was a description which shed some more light on the nature of the dissatisfaction which I had myself known. The sense of 'something wrong as I naturally stood' had certainly been experienced. The sense of need somehow to fill up 'that hole at the heart of things' had without a doubt come upon me with force.

It must have been considerable, because it was soon afterwards that I was driven to make a completely new start. The world of business knew me no more. I went home, there to draw up a programme of reading and study in order to remedy, as far as possible, the deficiencies of a neglected education. My parents were then living in Cardiff. To their house, then, I returned, being received with nothing but kindness, even though the failure of my first attempt at life was obvious. At the back of the house I made myself a study. Often in that room, late at night, I would hear the City hall clock strike the hours, and remind myself that near that clock was what for me had become a promised land—a university. This, a constituent college of the University of Wales, was, in fact, where I eventually arrived, and after graduating there I went to Oxford and repeated the process.

Yet it was all quite in vain, so far as the object of the whole exercise was concerned. For that object, after all, was to fill up by some means that 'hole at the heart of things.' It seemed to me that the material with which this cavity of meaninglessness could most satisfactorily be

filled was knowledge. And so I stuffed into it the accumu-
lated rubble of wide general reading. But the emptiness
persisted just the same. Like Omar Khayyam,

> Myself when young did eagerly frequent
> Doctor and Saint, and heard great argument
> About it and about, but evermore
> Came out by the same door as in I went.

It followed inevitably that, as regards the discovery of
any ultimate purpose in things, I was, towards the end
of my university career, no better off than I had been at
the beginning. I did, however, in those final years, at
least discover, or perhaps it would be more accurate to
say rediscovered, something else—the Church. The
details of how this came about have no particular relevance to this narrative. Let it be enough to say that one
evening, towards a long, anxious discussion with my
father as to what I should do with my life—neither he
nor I knew—he suggested I should take the problem to
the Vicar of the parish in which we lived. It was this man,
dead these many years, who set me on the road to ordination. A gruff, hard man, he had yet that inestimable
virtue in a priest of knowing exactly what he was doing,
of believing in what he was saying, and of having sound
professional competence in both. In his barrack-like
house, devoid of any grace or comfort, he lived like a
soldier on duty. Vigilant, unsentimental, he conducted
the routines of his profession with military precision,
reporting daily before the altar in his bleak church. For
some reason or other the mental image of him standing
there always seems to conjure up the words 'let a man so
account of us, as of the ministers of Christ, and stewards of
the mysteries of God.' Such men, perhaps, can never

know the effect they have on others. In the case of this man, he would probably in any event have been indifferent. He was doing his duty: that was enough. But his effect on me was powerful. He represented the Church: its mystery, its power: its ancient disciplines. Whether he represented Christ to me is another matter. But I had much reason to be grateful to him, even so. I began, under his influence, to believe that I had found, if not a way out of my perplexities, at any rate a signpost pointing to the way. It therefore seemed reasonable to suppose that, if I applied myself hard enough, like a man trying to pass an examination, to this business of religion, I should in due course penetrate its mysteries and learn to live the life of faith which seemed so admirable. If the results were meagre, as they were, it was, of course, only to be expected. There is, after all, no such thing as a 'do it yourself' Christianity. But I was then a long way from discovering this truth.

Meanwhile, a book come upon at this time, wonderful as it was, had a considerable effect in causing me to persist in this fundamental error—not even yet by any means wholly corrected—of supposing that salvation depended upon personal effort. This was William Law's *Serious Call to a Devout and Holy Life*. It has, of course, profoundly affected many. Johnson said he found it 'quite an over match' for him when, at Oxford, he came upon it for the first time. Even Gibbon had to say that 'a philosopher must allow that he exposes, with equal severity and truth, the strange contradiction between the faith and practice of the Christian world.' My error lay not so much in reading this book as in misreading it. 'How amazing,' Law exclaims, 'it is to see how eagerly men

employ their parts, their sagacity, time, study, application and exercise . . . when anything is devised or intended
in worldly matters, and how little they use their sagacity
and abilities to raise and increase their devotion!' Let a
man but apply himself to his religion with the same ardour
that he gives to his job when he wants to get on, Law
seemed to be saying, and considerable results will follow.
In my case they did not. A sombre determination to
persist in certain prefabricated, ecclesiastically inspired,
rules of life was soon all that was left of an enthusiasm
for holiness inspired by Law. If I had read the good man
more carefully this could have been avoided. The reason
is simple, he says, why some people 'make no greater
progress in that religion which they so much admire . . . it
is because religion lives only in their head, but something
else has possession of their heart.' But that again was
something I still had to learn.

So the motivation of my reaching out to the Church
at that time of my life was more one of self-preservation
than anything else. I saw the Church—and maybe the
image was not such a bad one—as a lighthouse shining
across waters both deep and dark. It seemed to be
that if I could get to that lighthouse, and if especially
I could live in it and even help to work the light, I should
at last and at least be doing something which had meaning
and be among people who knew what that meaning was.

All these suppositions, what is more, turned out to some
extent to be correct. I did get to the lighthouse. I came to
see that this light of the Christian faith was the only
one which seemed to have any effect upon the darkness
around. It has been shining a long time, all across the
centuries. It was very important. And therefore it
appeared that to help to maintain it was a proper use of

whatever time and talents one had. The Church, in fact, was that place, and that alone, in which meaning and purpose could be found, even though its external manifestations; its customs, inhibitions, its antiquated forms of expression, even often enough, its personnel, could be very trying to live with. It was at least all glorious within, an earthen vessel holding a treasure of truth. And it further appeared that, so far as I was concerned, the place for me, however arduous and distasteful the way there, was within the ministry of that Church. The intention was good; the purpose sincere.

Both were insufficient. One of the few comforts it is possible to find in the contemplation of such a fact is that the situation was by no means novel. There must have been many men who down the generations have sought ordination for any number of sound reasons while forgetting that the only really sensible one is the apparently mad wish to down tools and serve Christ merely because he happened to have passed by and looked at them, as befell Matthew busy with his tax-gathering, and Peter and Andrew when they were fishing. Short of this, there can still be many quite honourable motives for ordination. A desire to serve one's fellow-men in a more direct manner than would otherwise, as some, often mistakenly, imagine, be possible, is one of them. Others again may see in it an answer to personal perplexities, and a settling of doubts by moving into a situation where doubt, as is sometimes supposed, has to be sealed-off and buried, like radio-active waste. It is even possible to see along this particular road a way of life which appears agreeable. Certainly, numerous nice people can be encountered along this path. Literature is full of them. But Nemesis can also be encountered along that same path, quite possibly in the form of a sudden and unnerving revelation of inadequacy.

Something like this, I truly believe and must honestly say, was what happened to me. I was ordained deacon in the Cathedral Church of St. Peter, Bradford, on December 19th, 1937. The evening before there had occurred the third of those moments of truth of which I am now trying to tell.

An ordination retreat—that going apart into seclusion for some days before the event—is not necessarily a cheerful occasion. It can be, and probably should be, a severe test of resolution. The actual circumstances may be depressing. Close contact with any ecclesiastical machinery often is. Or a man may find himself in uncongenial company, perhaps in sharp contrast to gayer friends known elsewhere. And yet again the prospect of being about to take an irrevocable step into an ill-defined area of experience may weigh heavily upon the spirits. It was some such slight reasons as these that, on the Saturday evening of December 18th, I assembled together and charged with being the cause of the disquiet of which I was becoming increasingly conscious as the hours wore on. But they had to be acquitted: they were excuses; not causes. The cause of the disquiet lay in myself, in a sharp sense of inadequacy for what I was about to undertake, in a growing suspicion that I ought not to be undertaking it at all, and in a conviction experienced then for the first time, that the root of the whole trouble lay in the fact that I was trying, to a considerable extent for the wrong reasons, to make my own way along a path where, as a fact, only Christ could lead. It could all be put more simply by saying that I suddenly saw, or was shown, the truth about myself, and did not like it at all.

'Woe unto them,' says Isaiah, 'that seek deep to hide their counsel from the Lord, and their works are in the dark, and they say, who seeth me? And who knoweth us?'[1]

But the hour was late. What was to be done? As I sat in Chapel that evening listening to the last trams dolefully grinding up one of Bradford's many hills, it seemed that the one way left was to make an act of unconditional surrender to a Christ who, it now became clear, could be known at all in any depth of reality only if that surrender were made. This involved, it was clear, certain practical consequences, of which the chief was a willingness to be led. This in itself required a formidable change of mental attitude towards the whole matter of living one's life, a change away from the deeply ingrained notion that it was a man's first duty to make his own way privately, placing personal considerations first, towards a desire to try to serve Christ in situations where hitherto it had seemed perfectly natural to serve self. To quote Isaiah again: 'not doing thine own ways, nor finding thine own pleasure, nor speaking thine own words: then shalt thou delight thyself in the Lord.'[2]

But how did one make this act of surrender? It is impossible, as has been well said, to accept the fact of Jesus as Lord, in other words, as the dominating influence in one's life, without reference to a particular situation and his demands on us in it. This is surely the point at which so much emotional 'acceptance of Christ' runs into the sands. It means little because it demands little in terms of practical action. But when, on the contrary a man faced, say, with the break-up of his marriage, turns to

[1] Isaiah 29. 15.   [2] Isaiah 58. 13-14.

Christ for help, a very real change in his own inner dispositions will be demanded of him—a rooting out of his own antipathies, perhaps the overcoming of a tremendous desire, maybe even a true love, for another woman. Or, to take another instance, to bring Christ into a situation where racial tensions exist, the price to be paid, the action demanded, is a rooting out, sometimes with pain and difficulty, or personal prejudices before it becomes possible to act fruitfully in regard to those of others. Acceptance of Christ, in fact, inevitably lets us in for something. If it doesn't, there is something wrong.

In this present instance that was indeed the case. The price to be paid here, it seemed, was chiefly that of handing over to Christ that which had hitherto been the most jealously guarded of all personal possessions—the freedom to act in all circumstances on the basis of self-direction, and to replace this with a recognition of the duty to ask instead what Christ's direction would be, what his love would demand, in any given situation. This is, of course, extremely difficult, perhaps more so for some than others. For me, acceptance of the need for grace proved then, as indeed it has continued to prove, difficult because so much against the grain of one's nature. But the great thing was to make a beginning with that act of acceptance, and to go ahead in the faith that, as time went by, it would become fuller and richer, The central importance of this moment of truth lay just in that. It was a moment inaugurating a long battle for the conquest of self. And though, thus to try, many years later, to imprison in words the extremely elusive nature of the truth which was then revealed is to risk over-simplification, conclusions based on hind-sight, and all the rest of the dangers inherent in spiritual autobiography, yet of the central importance of the experience, in the light of what has subsequently developed from it, I have no doubt whatever. This was the way in which, at a specific time and place, Christ came to challenge me. The encounters of later years, with many other Christians of all sorts and conditions, have indicated that this is a kind of challenge and encounter happening far oftener than we think because hidden away in the intimacies of private lives. A well-known passage from Albert Schweitzer seems to contain the essence of the matter.

'He comes to us as one unknown, without a name, as of old, by the lake-side he came to those men who knew him not. He speaks to us in the same words: "Follow thou me," and sets us to the tasks which he has to fulfil for our time. He commands. And to those who obey him, whether they be wise or simple, he will reveal himself in the toils, the conflicts, the sufferings which they shall pass through in his fellowship, and, as an ineffable mystery, they shall learn in their own experience who he is.'

The immediate consequences of this moment of truth so far as I was concerned, was that it enabled me to go ahead, with a good heart and with honest intention, on the path which then lay before me. Here again, of course, the light that had shone about the moment soon diminished. The essence of the matter was that I now had a guiding light, the everlasting mercy of which cannot, it would seem, ever be fully appreciated until one has floundered around in the dark for a while. Repentance must precede forgiveness, and forgiveness must be followed by response. 'We love,' as St. John says, 'because he first loved us,' and that would seem to be about the heart of the matter. The fact that this small but intense experience befell on the eve of ordination was, of course, fortuitous. It would have been equally critical at any similar juncture of life in any calling. So it is equally fortuitous that this narrative happens to be concerned with a man whose particular destiny it has been to make such spiritual discoveries as have come his way within the context of the ministry. Nothing could be further from the purpose of this account than to suggest that Christ can be encountered more probably or more easily upon that road than upon any other. The very opposite can indeed sometimes be the case. The only point of any importance here is the truth which this humble little happening appears to suggest is that it is particularly when the soul feels really lost that Christ is most likely to reveal himself as a guide.

It was seven years before another moment of quite that intensity came along. Even then it was of an entirely different kind. And of course, in the meantime a great many things happened. But since this is a narrative of an inward journey rather than a tale of outward events it is of no relevance to mention them. Let it be sufficient to say, then, that the life which began for me on December 19th, 1937, proved to be unexpectedly rewarding, rich in undeserved opportunities of service, and of contacts with a few lives made beautiful by the faith shining through them. There were, inevitably, many difficulties, many points of tension. No doubt this always will be the case. It is to be expected that Christ's kindly light will in fact lead 'o'er moor and fen, o'er crag and torrent' as well as long easier ways. The one thing to fear is that the light will go out.

That never happened; but it would be untrue to say that it never sank low. It is true of the Christian life that 'they that do the work shall know the doctrine.' It is true that no one can honestly persist in it without, surely, learning something of 'what is the breadth and length and height and depth of the love of Christ' especially when his work takes him into the lives of others at an intimate level, as that of the ministry must do. And indeed this was found to be true enough, first in a parish among mills in the West Riding of Yorkshire, then in others in Kent, through the war years and afterwards. Yet, in terms of inner illuminations or revelations of further truth, the pace was pedestrian. This was particularly true of worship. It was easy enough to be dutiful about it: but to recome rapt, to be made aware through it of a mystery beyond, was rare indeed. Perhaps one reason why that passage in *Honest to God* in which the Bishop of Woolwich spoke of being surrounded, at his theological college, by all the apparatus of prayer and yet able to derive so little from it, touched a chord in so many minds, was because the reaction was a common, if unusually unacknowledged, one. It is always possible to compensate for this lack of what market research people would call 'consumer satisfaction' in the devotional side of the Christian life by saying we should not expect it.

Thus Evelyn Underhill in *The Fruit of the Spirit*: 'Faithfulness is consecration in overalls. It is the steady acceptance and performance of the common duty and immediate task . . . a lot of the road to heaven has to be taken at thirty miles an hour . . . whatever path we have to travel, in whatever department we are asked to serve, we soon realize that sturdy faithfulness alone will see us through. . . .'

True enough, no doubt. And always, of course, there were the meetings with Christ in his sacrament. When in later years, it fell to my lot to discover a good deal about

that remarkable priest, Geoffrey Studdert Kennedy—
to write his biography, in fact—one of the many stories
told of him which raised an immediate echo in the heart
was of how, being asked, as he returned from the battle
of Messines in the first world war, how he stood as regards
his beliefs after so traumatic an experience, he said that he
felt only Christ and his sacrament were left untouched;
but of them he felt absolutely sure. 'The Sacrament,'
he said elsewhere, 'is the heart, the blood centre, of the
great army of people who, having seen and loved God in
Christ, are resolved to fight for and suffer with him unto
death and beyond it.' Such has often been the Christian
experience. Many have 'known him in the breaking of
the bread.' But it has also been a part of the Christian
experience to yearn in addition for the occasional bright
moment in the round of dutiful worship which bathes
the whole affair for once in a light more extraordinary
than that of common day. From the church tower in
the parish of my first curacy, each noon the bells would
play the little tune of:

> Lead me Lord,
> Lead me in thy righteousness
> Make thy way plain
> Before my face.

I believed that he was doing so. But also, beyond a
doubt, I longed sometimes for a more direct revelation of
himself. It came within the course of an hour or so one
evening in the November of 1944.

The place was the undercroft of Canterbury Cathedral,
the occasion the eve of the funeral of Archbishop
William Temple. Following his sudden death—an event
big enough to shake much of Christendom, even in the

midst of war—the body had been brought to lie before the altar for that last night. So there, in that shadowed, infinitely peaceful, ancient place, all grey stone and silence, the coffin lay. Those who felt so disposed—and some who owed much to that great man did—could watch and pray there awhile. It seemed then that into the portentous quiet there came a very marked sense of the holy, an acute awareness of the 'other,' the supernatural, the beyond time and circumstance. Just as so much of what William Temple in his life had said and written had made sense out of the Christian mysteries, so now at his death it seemed that for a moment the same lucidity permitted a vision of the reality of spiritual things. This, one seemed to be being told, was what worship was all about. This was what was there all the time, behind and beyond all the words, all the arguments, all the gropings. One felt an inkling of the truth that Christ reveals himself at times through other channels than those of rational thought. He comes through the mystic and the inexplicable as well, although in our highly pragmatic western world we have become virtually tone-deaf to such other-worldly music. But, once heard, it is never forgotten.

The point is of importance. There are two tests which can be applied to any supposedly spiritual experience in order to discover whether it was anything other than a personal reaction to particular circumstances. The first is the test of continuance. Did this experience, this moment of truth, then, outlast the emotions of the moment? It did indeed. The sense of the elusive mystery behind the outer shell of worship has never since then wholly faded away. That which was encountered in the undercroft at Canterbury within the penumbra, as it were, of the spirit of a holy man, was, so far as this writer is concerned, the Lord manifesting himself in yet another of the many differing ways in which from time to time he chooses to do so. Today it may be through some challenge to love and service, tomorrow through a call to see him in the lonely; the day after he may come even in the guise of some difficult personality making demands upon time and patience. But sometimes also it would seem to be his good pleasure to come to us in perfect beauty, moving the astonished beholder to adore, like the disciples on the Mount of Transfiguration. This is the Christ who, to quote Studdert Kennedy again, is 'the kingdom, the power and the glory, the towers of York and Bach's Mass in B Minor,' a presence not to be apprehended through words and sense, because beyond either.

The second test might be called that of comparison. Have other men, especially wiser men, spoken of phenomena of a similar nature? If they have, and if a personal experience can be related to a larger body of truth, then considerable confidence can be felt in it. The reading of Rudolf Otto's classic *The Idea of the Holy* had that effect in this instance, placing this little personal experience— often since repeated—in a wide context. 'The feeling of the uncanny, the thrill of awe or reverence . . . the feelings of religious rapture and exaltation' are, he maintains, of the essence of the matter. They existed before religion became, as it has for so many of us, morality touched with emotion. They are of enormous importance. 'Let us consider,' he says in a notable passage, 'the deepest and most fundamental element in all strong and sincerely felt religious emotion. Faith unto salvation, trust, love—all these are there. But over and above these is an element which may also on occasion, quite apart from them, profoundly affect us and occupy the mind with a well-nigh bewildering strength. Let us follow it up with every effort of sympathy and imaginative intuition wherever it is to be found, in the lives of those around us; in sudden strong ebullitions of personal piety. . . . If we do so we shall find we are dealing with something for which there is only one appropriate expression, *mysterium tremendum*.'[1]

That surely is the essence of the many-sided Christ who comes into our lives in so many forms. It remains now to tell, so far as this brief account of one very ordinary man's spiritual journey is concerned, of one further revelation which can be identified in the course of it. This, however, cannot properly be called 'a moment of truth.' Like so much else which has not been told in this tale, it was rather part of gradual movement towards truth. But it did have a moment of beginning. That was when it fell to my lot, some years ago, to be involved in making a series of television programmes which had as their object the answering of the question 'does Christ, in this day and age, come into people's lives and change them?' It was perhaps some indication of many inner timidities and doubts, of, indeed, a weakness of faith, that at the beginning of the enterprise it seemed natural to assume that clearly verifiable instances, in contemporary lives, of what a former age would have without inhibitions called the saving power of Christ would be hard to come by. And yet the form of the programme required that actual persons should be found, and induced to come before the cameras to speak of what had befallen them in this respect.

[1] Rudolf Otto, *The Idea of the Holy*, Pelican Books.

C

The event proved all hestitations to have been needless. Indeed, it was necessary only to go out into the highways and byways in order to find in many lives clear evidences of the continuing miracle of the Christ encounter. An extraordinary variety of people eventually came to take part in the programme. Some, such as the writers Arthur Calder-Marshall and Hugh Redwood, Douglas Hyde the ex-communist, Father Potter of Peckham, the unforgettable Franciscan, were already well-known people. Others, such as a Japanese woman who was a schoolgirl in Hiroshima the day the bomb fell and who learned forgiveness through suffering, were unknowns who came, bravely made their testimonies, and went their way. Yet all had shared a common experience—the direct intervention of God in their lives in various circumstances and in many different ways.

Some of the narratives were later gathered together in a book,[1] a passage from the introduction to which has relevance here: 'People experience God in many forms. ... In the Christian life, it is quite possible to go on quietly for a long time and then suddenly, in some situation of need or challenge, to encounter very dramatically indeed the God in whom one has believed all along ... God does unmistakably from time to time break into people's lives with compelling force. . . . If God did not thus declare himself then religion, which is in essence a seeking for communion with God, would be a sadly one-sided affair, with men and women doing all the seeking without ever receiving that profound, heart-warming, indeed electrifying experience which comes from finding.'

Heart-warming and electrifying indeed! The effect of thus meeting with people who were living testimonies to

[1] *This Is My Story*, Hodder & Stoughton.

the reality of the Christ encounter here and now was both those things. It is noted here as the latest in a series of little moments of truth which have befallen in the course of the journey which has been here outlined. They have been stages, I firmly believe, in a gentle and continuing disclosure by Christ of himself, always in a form and manner which could be understood. The effect, of course, is total: not in making a saint out of a sinner; but in making a sinner convinced that his sins matter, and that he whom he knows now as a friend will also be his judge. No doubt, in the fullness of time, perhaps at the end of this earthly journey, there will be other disclosures of truth. Meanwhile, it is very much to feel able to say, as regards this Christ, not indeed that one understands a fraction of his mystery so much as that one has experienced his life-changing love and can say, like the man in St. John whom the Lord, to Pharisaic indignation, healed on the Sabbath: 'All I know is this: once I was blind, now I can see.'

4. *This Happened to Me*

CUTHBERT BARDSLEY

IN DIFFERING ways Christ makes himself known to men. To some he comes suddenly. To others he comes so quietly and gently that it is only long afterwards that the person concerned can say 'that was the voice of God.' To some he makes himself known in a single experience of conversion: to others, awakening to his claims is a steady progress towards awareness, as described in the previous chapter of this book.

My experience falls somewhere between the two. Despite—or perhaps because of—a secure, comfortable homelife, I needed to be awakened from the half existence of the complacent and fortunate, with no problems or difficulties, moral or intellectual.

My father was Vicar of Lancaster, and it was in that town that I spent most of the first twenty-five years of my life. As a small boy I would lie awake at night listening to the expresses roaring over the viaduct, going north or south. My small mind would conjure up the mysterious romance of those distant places, and even in those early years there was born in my heart the keen desire to travel which has been at the centre of my make-up ever since.

The other memory of those innocent childhood days is, oddly enough, of my father's boots which, like black boats, lay nightly outside his bedroom door. I can still hear the thud as he forced on the wooden trees, banging the boots on the floor to enable the trees to be inserted. Slowly my eyes would travel upwards from these vast boots to the owner of them. He had a kindly face; tanned, surmounted by brown hair showing few streaks of grey—a face dominated by the eyes—humorous, compassionate, penetrating.

Every morning I would hear him walk past my room to the bathroom. Afterwards, I would watch him shave, then go over to the church for Matins. Morning by morning I sat in my accustomed pew in the war memorial chapel, listening. That done, we walked, often hand in hand, down the hill to breakfast. Then he would go to his study with its green baize door to keep out the sounds of children. Only rarely did I penetrate there, to see its array of books, its vast desk where sat my father on his swivel chair. On my arrival he would at once, if free, move to a large armchair. Sitting on his knee, I would be asked about my day, what I had been doing, my plans for the future, my difficulties or problems. And then he would begin to talk about the future, filling me with a sense of enthusiasm for what lay ahead of me. With his gay laugh and the wave of the arm with which he would dismiss possible difficulties, he would communicate to all who met him a zest and buoyant hope for the future before which all difficulties seemed to disappear like morning mist before the sun. It was there, on my father's knee, that I was first introduced, perhaps subconsciously, to the challenges and joys of a parish priest's life. It was there that he first revealed to me his ardent hope that I would follow in his footsteps. And yet it has to be said that conflict arose in my heart on this point. Love for, and admiration of, my father made me long to do as he wished. But love of the world made me instinctively wish to cling onto the easy pleasures of the life to which I was accustomed.

I could almost set my watch by the moment when my father left his study for an afternoon's visiting. It was precisely at two-thirty. At five he would return for tea. Then over tea, he would talk of his experiences, and I came to build up slowly a picture of a much loved parish priest who was welcome everywhere, who listened daily to many problems, and who by sanctified common sense was able to help with many. Yet the sense of the isolation and set-apartness of such a life still, among other things, held me back from wishing to follow him in it.

So for twenty-one years I grew up in the atmosphere of a delightful, comfortable, well-appointed home. Day after day I was influenced by the regular recitation of grace at meals, Matins before breakfast, Matins and Evensong on Sunday. These Sunday services were a high water mark in my life, for they took place in a large, very beautiful Parish Church, where the congregation seemed enormous, especially at night; the choir was effective, the congregational singing hearty. I can still smell the atmosphere of warm clothes, candlegrease—a sort of indescribable, rather fusty, holiness which seems to belong to so many ancient churches. I loved it and looked forward to it week by week. Here was Anglican piety at its best; unspectacular, unemotional, undemanding, but quietly impressive and character-forming. And all the time I enjoyed the reflected glory of my father's sanctity and my mother's piety. Inevitably I was influenced— who could not have been—by the atmosphere of such a home and church, and to a lesser extent by the schools to which I went. But that was all.

And then the blow fell: the whole fortunate idyll came to an end. In the summer of 1928 I was rowing for my college at Henley Regatta. My father came to see our crew row on the Thursday. On the Sunday I drove home, looking forward to the Long Vacation. All the way north I savoured the many pleasures ahead: golf, tennis, swimming, travel. About tea-time I neared my home. Passing along the street I thought one or two people eyed me strangely, but thought nothing of it. But when I entered the house it was to find that my father had died that morning.

I am not for a moment claiming any uniqueness about this event. Sudden death comes to many families. All I am saying—and even then only because this death was a turning-point in my life, and so has an importance in this personal narrative of that life—that never before had anything affected me so profoundly. It was as though I had grown up in the space of a few minutes. Till then I had been the fortunate youth—perhaps too fortunate, leaning perhaps too much upon a wiser and stronger personality. Now he was gone, and I was the one to whom the family turned. Outwardly I carried on. Inwardly I felt cold, wondering, as did Matthew Arnold about his father,

> '. . . by what shore
> Tarriest thou now? For that force,
> Surely, has not been left vain!
> Somewhere, surely, afar,
> In the sounding labour-house vast
> of being, is practised that strength,
> Zealous, beneficent, firm!'

Five days later there took place his funeral. The church was packed. The streets were thronged, with people standing four deep and some of the shops closed in honour of a man whom so many had come to know, to love, and to value. It was then, on the way home from this funeral, that I knew beyond all doubt that I had to do as he had wished. The doubts and uncertainties I had had vanished away. The Lord spoke to me that day, I am sure, by revealing to me both how much my father had been loved and by showing me thereby how useful the life of a parish priest could be. I saw in many sad faces that day expressions of gratitude to this one man. True, he had not been distinguished—as the world would recognize distinction. He had not been a scholar, nor an orator, nor a highly skilled administrator. But he had been a pastor who knew and was known by his sheep. And I felt with absolute certainty that I must carry on his work.

But how?

It was one thing to be moved emotionally in this way. It was another to find where I was really equipped to travel this particular road. Had I sufficient faith? Did I really believe in God? As time passed after my father's death, I felt very much alone: confused and lost. It was a difficult time.

C. S. Lewis, whose book *A Grief Observed* impressed me much, writing after the death of his wife, outlined a state of mind to which my own at this juncture bore, I think, some resemblance:

'Feelings, and feelings, and feelings. Let me try thinking instead. From the rational point of view, what new factor has H.'s death introduced into the problem of the universe? What grounds has it given me for doubting all that I believe? I knew already that these things, and worse happened daily. I would have said that I had taken them into account. I had been warned—I had warned myself—not to reckon on worldly happiness. We were even promised sufferings. They were part of the pro-gramme. We were even told "Blessed are they that mourn," and I accepted it. I've got nothing that I hadn't bargained for. Of course it is different when the thing happens to oneself, not to others, and in reality, not in imagination. Yes, but should it, for a sane man, make quite such a difference as this? No. And it wouldn't for a man whose faith had been real faith and whose concern for other people's sorrows had been real concern. The case is too plain. If my house had collapsed at one blow, that is because it was a house of cards. The faith which "took these things into account" was not faith but imagina-tion. The taking them into account was not real sympathy. If I had really cared, as I thought I did, about the sorrows of the world, I should not have been so over-whelmed when my own sorrow came.'[1]

In October I returned to Oxford. There began for me, I believe, out of all this grief, and all the desire to have a fuller capacity for the service of God and man to which it had given rise, what I can describe only as a time of the deepening of life. This showed itself, first and foremost, in a series of significant personal relationships of a nature that I had not known before.

One day, I met a man whose unselfconscious humility and gentleness drew me to him. Quite naturally he began to talk about his faith, and it was abundantly clear to me that his was more real to him than mine was to me. He began to talk about Christ as no one had ever

[1] C. S. Lewis, *A Grief Observed*, Faber & Faber.

C*

talked to me before, as of one who could guide and mould
a man's life. I told him that I would like to see him again.
And so a few days later I found myself walking with
increasingly hesitant steps towards his house. Deep in my
heart I knew that something drastic was about to take
place, something that was going to change my life. But
I was not at all sure that I wanted it to be changed.
Or did I? I was unhappy: lonely and dissatisfied. My
own religious disciplines, though maintained, had been
becoming increasingly unreal and unsatisfying. I was
missing my father grievously, and was puzzled about my
future.

On arrival at his home we talked. He told me more
about Christ, and how he could satisfy all needs, bring
help to weaknesses, forgiveness for sins. I knew that my
faith in comparison with this standard was weak and
flabby—that God was remote, impersonal, unreal,
despite all that my father and mother had taught me.
There was an essential element missing—that of full
personal commitment to Christ.

After a long, unhurried conversation I knelt down.
Unemotionally—indeed in a somewhat matter-of-fact
way—I accepted Jesus Christ as Lord, feeling sure of his
forgiveness for my sins of commission and omission, and
asking for his strength to make me a finer and more
courageous Christian. Then I remember I waited—
relaxed and receptive—to see if there was anything he
would have me to do forthwith. At once the answer
came. I was reminded of an incident that had occurred
a few months before when I was rowing. I had found
myself sharing a bedroom with three other men. Hitherto, from the ingrained habit of a lifetime, I had always
knelt down to say my prayers before going to sleep. But

this time I had hesitated. The arguments against seemed unassailable. I should be doing more harm than good. I should be regarded as religiously exhibitionist. I should be bringing an unnatural reticence into an otherwise gay and amusing party. So I had gone to bed without further pause. The same thing occurred the following evening. On the third my conscience disturbed me, however—so much that, when I had thought the others were all asleep, I got out of bed, knelt down, said my prayers as always. This incident I had entirely forgotten, but in the course of the interview it came back to my mind, and with it the thought that here had been an act of both cowardice and concealment which now, under the new dispensation of which I had become conscious, a new intensity of obedience to Christ in small things as in great, was no longer to be tolerated. It seemed to me therefore that I was called upon, however embarrassing it may be, to apologize to one of those men. Fortunately I knew that I seldom saw him, so put it out of my mind and went back to my room.

And yet the following morning, as I was walking down a road in Oxford, the man I had in mind came into view. I remember a feeling of momentary panic as he approached. And then, without pause, I told him exactly what was on my mind, ending, as I had resolved, with an apology. There was a long silence. And then he made an unexpected reply. 'I, too, owe you an apology, for I also had the same thoughts that night.' And I had not known that he was a Christian.

Thus recounted, many years later, the incident may well seem trivial. It may even seem out of key with the great theme of how and when Christ enters into the lives of men. But, so far as I am personally concerned, and especially in the light of what has happened in my life since, it is not so. We have no warrant whatever for supposing that God speaks with us only on great generalized issues, or through events divorced from the minutiae of personal life. The very opposite is the case. The picture which the gospels give of Christ show him as ever ready to be involved with the small things of everyday, and indeed to speak to men and women through them. It is in the local and the particular that we can meet him. A part of his humanity is that he is concerned with our humanity, in all its smallness. There is joy in heaven, he asssures us, over *one* sinner who repents: one person, one individual. We may fairly assume, therefore, that one victory in one little life, is now, and always will be, of greater value than any number of generalized good intentions which do not involve personal action. There have been many men and women who, having once served Christ in small things, have gone on from that point to serve him in larger, having been assured, by that contact, that he is there, and that he cares. Some words from the parable of the talents have an application here, surely, even though it may not be a customary one. A man going on a journey entrusts his servants with certain funds. On his return he calls them to account. To the one who has done his best with what he had he says: 'Well done, my good and trusty servant! You have proved trustworthy in a small way: I will put you in charge of something big.'[1] As regards this small incident in my own young life, I can only record then, as a fact, that it did lead on to much.

[1] Matthew 25. 21.

All at once the light seemed to come on in the house of my life. I knew that God was there, that it was he who had led me to make this apology, that it was he who had given me the strength to say what had to be said. From that moment my faith deepened, became more experiential. I had been introduced to a living Lord who appeared to be interested in the little happenings of my uneventful life. It was, as I have said, a beginning. Up till then Christ had been the pattern of a good life, which I had seen reflected in my father, something to be admired from afar. The notion that God would speak to me in this intimate way had never entered my mind. He had been remote. But from then on I began to experience him in the depths of my being.

Years ago it was sometimes possible to find a framed text hanging on the wall in old-fashioned households which went something like this: 'Christ is the head of this house: the silent guest at every meal, the unseen listener to every conversation.' I have always felt there was something of great value in the idea there expressed in homely fashion—the idea of Christ with us always. It made a great difference to me.

Almost immediately things began to happen. I became aware of my neighbours, seeing them in a new light, as people with problems; the lonely, the frightened, the tempted. With this awareness came the desire to help them by introducing them to the Lord who had become so real to me.

One day, shortly after this, I encountered quite by chance, it appeared, a man whom I knew only slightly. He was a scholar of the first class intellectually, rather remote in manner. He commented, rather airily, that I was looking unusually happy. Briefly I told him why.

At the time he said little, but some months later, after my ordination, he accompanied my vicar and I on a journey to the Continent. His presence with us at all was surprising. A few days before I had been strongly moved inwardly to ask him to join us. Much to my surprise he had accepted my invitation. On the boat, as we crossed the Channel, I noticed him having a long conversation with my vicar. I did not know until later that that conversation saved this young man from suicide; for it transpired that he had accepted my invitation, fully determined to end his life by throwing himself overboard on the journey. He had felt, for reasons which need not be revealed, that he could face life no longer. Chance? Or was there in all this a guiding hand to be seen? I did not know. But the incident brought into my life a new seriousness, for it taught me that we are responsible for one another, that we cannot take one another for granted, and that even in such sombre depths God was prepared to use for his purposes even a newly awakened, immature Christian like myself.

Today these may well seem small matters—no doubt they are so—but I have learned, as I have said, that the small matters *do* matter and that Christ is interested in the minutiae of our lives. No doubt our Lord's disciples spent much time talking to him about very simple and mundane affairs, but he appears to have been as much interested in them as in the greater issues. We have always to remember that our affairs are evaluated, not so much by their magnitude as by their quality.

So these little happenings meant much to me, for they underlined my new discovery of a living, loving God, who could speak, guide, forgive, and enable. The Lord had ceased to be remote, dwelling in a light inaccessible, and had become for me one who could enter, and influence my life profoundly through small things into greater—or what we are pleased to think are greater.

Since then my life's road has passed over hills and valleys, through scenery beautiful and squalid. I have experienced joy and happiness, sadness and suffering. But throughout that journey, undertaken in company with other wholehearted Christians, I have found that the truths revealed to me in the day of small beginnings have remained equally true in the day of big things, and that the Lord who led me to himself when I was a child still leads me as a man.

As is so often the case, St. Paul sums up the matter: 'When I was a child, my speech, my outlook and my thoughts were all childish. When I grew up, I had finished with childish things. Now we see only puzzling reflections in a mirror, but then shall we see face to face. My knowledge now is partial; then it will be whole, like God's knowledge of me.' But I would certainly claim that my faith now, as it was then, is essentially simple, and I would not have it otherwise. May it ever be, in fact, like the faith of those whom Whittier wrote of:

> In simple trust like their's who heard,
> Beside the Syrian Sea,
> The gracious calling of the Lord,
> Let us, like them, without a word
> Rise up and follow thee.

Today, in my fifties, I bear, I suppose, a fairly heavy burden of responsibility, but I still know, as clearly as I did thirty years ago, that 'My grace is sufficient for thee; my strength is made perfect in weakness.'

As I draw towards the latter years of my life I ask myself often what sort of Lord he is to whom thus I gave my life as a young man; and who called me into his service. Certainly he is one who encourages and inspires. But he is often stern—sitting in judgement on my failures, which are many, as I know he knows. He is not protective. But he is one who never lets one down, or lets one go, or, let it be said, lets one off.

But always and always I thank him for his compassion. This Master, who was himself 'acquainted with grief' is able to console and comfort us in our sorrows. Many have found this. So have I. When my youngest sister died at the age of twenty-six I was inconsolable. After my father's death, she had been a close companion, gay and vital. Suddenly, she was stricken. Within days she was dead. Before the funeral, I went into a village church to mourn, and be alone. A long time I sat there, deeply distressed. And then—quite suddenly and unemotionally, I knew that he was there, comforting and encouraging. There took place in that church in fact, an encounter with the risen Lord which has often put me in mind of the experience of Mary Magdalen in the garden. I knew that my Redeemer lived, and because of that, that my sister lived. Many a time, in trying to comfort others in a similar situation, I have drawn upon this experience and remembered in connection with it, some more words from *A Grief Observed.*[1]

'Suddenly, at the very moment when, so far, I mourned H. least, I remembered her best. Indeed it was something (almost) better than memory; an instantaneous, unanswerable impression. To say it was like a meeting would

_____
[1] C. S. Lewis, *A Grief Observed*, Faber & Faber.

be going too far. Yet there was that in it which tempts one to use those words. It was as if the lifting of the sorrow removed a barrier. . . . And so, perhaps, with God. I have gradually been coming to feel that the door is no longer shut and bolted. Was it my own frantic need that slammed it in my face? The time when there is nothing at all in your soul except a cry for help may be just the time when God can't give it: you are like a drowning man who can't be helped because he clutches and grabs. Perhaps your own reiterated cries deafen you to the voice you hoped to hear.'

And what of this Lord as an encourager, an enthuser, and a guide? Often indeed has he come to me in such a guise. When confronted by some difficult assignment or decision, I have remembered the phrase, 'I can't, but God can, through me.'

I could—as no doubt plenty of others could—recall many instances of this guiding, encouraging and enabling aspect of the experiencing of Christ. Any crowded life in his service is bound to be rich in them. But I will, for my part, select only three. The first belongs to the years when, as a young man, I became Rector of Woolwich in wartime. Among other industrial complexes in the parish was a factory employing 12,000 people. No clergyman had ever gone through the gates. I thought one should. I thought I should. But to say that the prospect was daunting is to put it mildly. To be of any use to any or the men in there required, in the first place, acceptance, and in the teeth of the inherited prejudices of the sadly many years in which Church and industry have had nothing to say to each other. How this prejudice was overcome—not by me, but by the good Lord—and how the work there, in the fullness of time, came to be rich contacts, and love and mutual regard, does not belong to this narrative. But what does is the fact—and it is here recorded as a fact—that whereas I began with a sense of total inadequacy for so formidable a task, I was enabled to go forward into it in a power which was clearly not my own. This is the point I am stressing here: not that the work was original or, maybe, in itself particularly difficult: but that for me it was, at the outset, very difficult indeed. But Christ, as I believe, strengthened my weakness, pardoned my inadequacies, and led me by the hand into a sphere of work much less explored and developed then, if I may say so, than now.

It was the same when I was asked, a little later on, to be Provost of Southwark Cathedral. Here again the prospect was daunting. The place was bomb-gutted and forlorn. Plastic covering empty windows flapped in the wind. Outside the noise of trains was almost deafening. Even a smell of cheese from a nearby factory pervaded the vestries. A small congregation occupied the front pews of the nave. Everything was in need of fresh paint, and the congregation was in need of new hope. And yet, and yet, the place came to life, though not through me at all; but through this same enabling power of Christ.

One day, shortly after my arrival, I was joined by a priest, the Reverend Colin Cuttell, now Vicar of All Hallows, Barking-by-the-Tower in the City of London. We met accidentally—or so it seemed—in the street. When I discovered that he was home from Canada, I asked him if he would like to tackle a job which had come into my mind as a means of making contact with the people around. I told him that I was looking for somebody who would visit the offices and warehouses in the vicinity of the Cathedral. So he began, and it was all very difficult. We had no hall, no office, not much spare money, few people. So we prayed, and in the middle of our prayers, a name flashed into my mind—the name of a retired admiral who was one of the heads of a large firm in the locality. Him we interviewed, and within two days were given free accommodation for the purpose we had in mind. That was the turning point, and from that moment on things improved, as day by day we sought the leading of the Holy Spirit and the grace of God. The South London Industrial Mission sprang from this small beginning.

And then again—and this is the third instance of experience of the enabling power of Christ of which I am trying to speak—there was the time when, after the war, I was asked to visit the army in the British Zone of occupied Germany to seek for ordination candidates. This turned out to be a very difficult and testing assignment. It has sometimes been said that in the modern world, and certainly in this country, anybody, in any position of authority, however humbly exercised or even unwillingly assumed, is somehow guilty until he is proved innocent. There is, as it were, a built-in resistance to whatever emanates from such a source. When to this had to be added in this case the atmosphere of anti-climax, of exhaustion after great effort, of impatience with a discipline which war had justified but which peace often rendered nearly intolerable—familiar features of any army of occupation the chief consideration of most of the members of which was, understandably, to get out of the army and go home—it was scarcely surprising that such a task as mine turned out to be formidable. I was received with courtesy; but there were moments of acute loneliness and embarrassment. There were also times of major

opportunity and decision. It was the question of a certain
Commander-in-Chief, in the course of a somewhat
rigorous interview, as to what I thought of the general
state of morale at that time—I told him I thought it bad—
which led to the inception of training courses in the basic
elements of the Christian faith, which continued thereafter
for a long time, and reached into many corners of the
world where British forces were to be found. In the course
of the eight and a half years during which they continued
many thousands of men must have attended them.

But this was but one incident. The main thing is that,
little by little then, in the not very easy situation of those
early days, the love of God and the power of God worked
marvellously. As always it is individuals; the fruit of the
Spirit ripening in people's lives as a result of some moment
of truth in the course of such an enterprise as this which we
remember long after the circumstances which gave rise
to it have passed away. So, though that British Army of
Occupation of over twenty years ago has this long time
been scattered to the winds; though the men of it are now
middle-aged, or old, or dead; yet the young man who
came late one night to my room, asking for help to find
God, as he put it, is still a keen memory. So is the Colonel
—now a country parson, much loved and faithful—then
at the height of his powers as a soldier, who came, very
humbly to offer himself in Christ's service. His was a
wonderful humility, putting one in mind of that Roman
officer in Matthew who asked Jesus, with total trust, to
heal his son. 'Sir, who am I to have you under my roof?
You need only say the word, and the boy will be cured.
I know, for I am myself under orders, with soldiers under
me.' It would be easy enough to add to the list of such:
bright and reassuring moments in a work which was always

arduous, sometimes very difficult. And now, when I meet men, as indeed I often do, who say they remember one of such visits of mine to a unit of theirs, I feel very rewarded and very humble.

But neither that, nor any other of these by-products of this experience with the forces is the reason why this matter is mentioned here. That there are dangers of considerable misunderstanding in speaking of it at all is obvious enough, of which the chief is of seeming to seek to put on record some personal achievement. Nothing could be further from either the truth or the intention. I am not aware, here or elsewhere, of having succeeded in anything: only of having tried hard. The truth is that, to be personal—which no one likes being; but this is a personal narrative—I am fully conscious that neither in this situation, nor in any of the others of major test in which life has placed me could I ever have survived without the enabling power of Christ. The intention is to say so. This I must dwell upon, because it is of the essence of my faith and my life. There is a simplicity here which we abandon, or smile at, or argue ourselves out of, at our peril. We must trust Christ, or not seek to walk with him at all. And trust must involve relying upon him in particular situations, to the limit, to lift us up, and make us capable of actions in his name of which, unaided, we should be quite incapable. This is not a matter of the will or the intelligence, so much as a willing surrender of the heart and mind to Christ in the full trust that he will never let us down; but always hold us up. It is an essential element of encounter with him; to move in his service boldly into situations in which one knows that alone one would be lost.

Evelyn Underhill has expressed it well: 'Christ never suggests that it is necessarily the most efficient, intelligent or fully developed person who is most fit for eternal life, or most pleasing to God—that is one of the most foolish illustrations of the natural man. His thoughts are not our thoughts: nor his values our values. It is far better, says Christ, to go lame and blind into heaven than to be very capable and clear-sighted and sure of yourself, to make others stumble, and end on the rubbish heap. The only thing that counts, and proves the presence of divine life in us, is total dedication to God, total dependence on him. . . . We have to become as little children, says Christ. He seems to assume it will take a lot of doing, and it does. It means measuring our smallness and weakness against the greatness of God, grasping the babyish quality of even our greatest achievements, and accepting the situation with delight.'[1]

It is a long time now since these events of which I have been speaking: my father's death, and the spiritual development which came out of it: the early days of my ministry, the testing and formative times of Woolwich and Southwark and of many other experiences of which I have not written and do not intend to. And of course, since then a great many events, small and great, have come my way. The consecration of my own Coventry Cathedral in 1962 may fairly be accounted, I suppose, an occasion of some magnitude. It was certainly an occasion of much test. So also have been the manifold duties, perhaps in these days more pressing and at the same time more difficult than they have ever been, of a diocesan Bishop. 'Hold up the weak, heal the sick, bind up the

---

[1] Evelyn Underhill, *The Fruits of the Spirit*, Longmans.

broken, bring again the outcasts, seek the lost. Be so merciful that you be not too remiss: so minister discipline, that you forget not mercy——.' So runs a passage in the form of the consecration of a bishop. It is a longish time, now, since I heard them in reference to myself. But time has not lessened the difficulties of constantly trying to carry out such splendid directives amid the harsh realities of life as it is.

But always there is this: the great truth, the great thread running through all, the reality of the Christ encounter, that, once accepted as Lord and Saviour, he is there for ever, enabling 'with perpetual light, the dullness of our blinded sight.' Often and often I have found the accuracy of the words: 'In the hour it shall be told you what you shall say.' And perhaps more often, and more searchingly I have been made to know, the truth of the words which came to Paul when he longed to be free of a disability which he felt within himself. 'My grace is all you need; power comes to its full strength in weakness.'

5. *These have helped Us*

WE HAVE spoken a good deal in these pages so far of this 'reality of the Christ encounter.' To do so, indeed, is the purpose of this book. Thus we have said that 'the need for a God who may be personally encountered, whom we can know and who we can feel knows us, does not grow less. On the contrary, it grows more acute as our own world becomes increasingly impersonal. . . . The possibility of encounter with this personal Christ, who down the ages has marvellously made himself known to men and women, is that which, we believe, beyond all else now can bring reassurance to those many who are feeling it hard either to persist in or to discover a living faith.'

It is time now to take this further. A phrase such as 'Christ encounter' is easy to use, much more difficult to define. What do we mean by it? We have tried to some extent to indicate an answer by looking at the matter in the lives of some saints, some mystics, and in those of some to whom he has come unrecognized. Last and very much least, as instances of progressive revelations of himself in the lives of two ordinary men, we have tried, out of a sense of duty rather than inclination, to look at our own very ordinary experiences. Yet there is more to be said concerning the manner and the consequences of that encounter in the lives of some people whom we have met, and who have greatly helped us, in our personal pilgrimages, by being so clearly among those of whom it could be said that men 'took note of them, that they had been with Jesus.' It may well be that such an exercise will help to bring us closer to at any rate a working definition of what we mean by 'encounter with Christ.'

'No one has ever seen God,' John bluntly says. True, he goes on to state that 'God's only son, he who is nearest to the father's heart, he has made him known.'[1] But when we ask ourselves how in fact he has made him known to us personally we come at once upon the startling fact that Christ has been shown to us, time and time again, through other people. Maybe the realization should not be so startling. Christ's people are his body: he has no other. 'I am the vine, and you are the branches.'[2] Even so, this naked fact that we see him, when we do see him, most memorably reflected in human lives of a particular order and quality, is a sharp reminder of how utter is the self-imposed dependence of the Lord upon those who are his witnesses from age to age.

But what is the particular order and quality of the Christ-centred life? It is important here to recognize the marked difference between the 'good' life, in the sense of the virtuous, righteous, high-principled, humanitarian-motivated life, and that which is consciously Christ centred. To fail to make that distinction is to fall into that same error which has done more than most to vitiate this whole matter—the error of supposing that the Christian life and the 'good' life are necessarily the same thing. The logical consequence of that is, ultimately, to come to consider the former as an unnecessary appendage of the latter. But it is not so. Love, joy, peace, patience, kindness, goodness, faithfulness, humility and self-control are the fruit of the Spirit in any age. They are the shining virtues. But there is another element in some Christian

[1] John 1. 18.   [2] John 15. 15.

lives which belongs less to the area of virtue as to that of religious experience: the element of power. The character is fundamentally altered by the Christ encounter, as a piece of clay alters shape under the hands of the potter, becoming something totally other, usually much more beautiful, and is enabled to reach far higher levels of moral and spiritual attainment than would otherwise have been the case.

This is, after all, the pattern of Pentecost. Those few people upon whom the Spirit came, changed by that experience; were empowered to a strength of witness hitherto denied them. 'I will endue even my slaves, both men and women, with a portion of my spirit,' Peter quotes Joel to prove to the astonished beholders of this phenomenon that it has behind it the warrant and the promise of Scripture. Both still hold: the experience of Pentecost is repeated in many forms in all ages, including our own. One of these forms is this changing and strengthening of human personality. It is a thing given, coming from without upon those who experience it. And it is this quality which seems to have been the hallmark of those of whom we wish to write here: not only because they have helped us in such spiritual pilgrimages as we have tried to make; but because, albeit in different ways and measures, they have manifested in their lives Christ working through the Holy Spirit. And insofar as they have done so, they are of importance to the purpose of showing something of the constant possibility of, and the constant miracle of, the Christ encounter today as yesterday. It may have been gathered, from an earlier chapter of this book in which the attempt was made to sketch the outlines of such tenuous inner development as has been this particular writer's, that no mention was made

of encounters of quite this order until near the end of
the narrative. This may have been chance. Alternatively,
it may have reflected a feeling that personalities unmistakably Christ centred and permeated were so improbable
as scarcely to warrant the seeking in the ordinary paths
of life. We tend to find, all of us, what we are looking for.
And if we expect to find nothing the expectation is likely
to be gratified. It was only when a longing grew for a
more direct revelation of Christ after many years of con-
scientious if pedestrian service of him that encounters
began to take place with people in whom evidences of this
presence were apparent.

The first such encounter one of us had was with a man
who had been dead more than thirty years when it took
place. The term may seem strange in such a context; but
it is the only one which seems adequate either to the
richness of the experience or to the consequences which
flowed from it. It all began with a name casually noticed,
in the curiosity of a passing moment on a memorial in
Worcester Cathedral—the name of a man never met in
the flesh—Geoffrey Studdert Kennedy. 'A poet, a
prophet, a passionate seeker after truth.' So the words
on the tablet described him. They stirred a faint recol-
lection, no more. Was not this the same man who had
written that poem somewhere of how Christ once crucified
on Calvary, had in aftertimes longed for a repetition of
the same fate instead of the indifference which faced him
in any modern city whenever he attempted to come
again into the hearts of men?

When Jesus came to Birmingham they simply passed him by.
They never hurt a hair of him, they only let him die—

The crowds went home and left the streets without a soul to see,
And Jesus crouched against a wall and cried for Calvary.

The idea hung in the mind, leading on to a curiosity concerning the originator of it. Who was he? What had he done, in his time and generation, to move men to put up this memorial to him? Even its phraseology was different from the usual, all too numerous, all too forgotten, memorials to the worthy dead of other days; the eminent citizens, the soldiers commemorated in deeds as dusty as they. 'A poet, a prophet, a seeker after truth.' The lines had a ring about them evocative of some once deeply felt emotion, suggesting that the man concerned had been more than the writer of some faintly recollected verse more notable for the originality of its idea than for any literary excellence. This indeed turned out to be the case. There was proved in that moment the truth of the words the writer of Hebrews used of Abel 'through faith he continued to speak after his death.' A curiosity to know more of the writer was born at that time which led ultimately, after some years of research into the origins, the background and the story of this 'poet, prophet, seeker after truth' to the uncovering from under the layers of the years of a truly Christ-permeated life. The experiencing of following the time-overgrown tracks he had made through the thickets of the life of his times was curious. Here was a man, it appeared, who had touched many people in an odd way; not by being particularly powerful or successful—he considered himself, in fact, a failure—as by speaking to them, as much by what he was as by what he said, of the reality of God in Christ.

The facts about this man can soon be told. An Irishman, an Anglican priest, it was his destiny to be caught up in the war of 1914–18, and to have in the course of it his faith tested to the uttermost. He emerged from it with a considerable fame, and a well-nigh broken heart,

THESE HAVE HELPED US 87

convinced that only in Christ could the sins and follies of
mankind be redeemed. He went on, in the decade after
that old war, to what Archbishop William Temple
described as 'a wonderful decade of prophecy,' becoming
in the course of it an orator of genius, listened to wherever
he went because he had so markedly, it seemed, a message
for his day and age. And always, in whatever context he
spoke, his theme was Christ the Lord of all life. And in
much exhausting personal counselling he was able to show
something of the love and wisdom of that Christ to many
entangled in the griefs, the bitternesses and the needs of a
gaunt period of history. Finally, worn-out, despairing—
in that as in so much else hauntingly like the Master whom
he tried to serve—he died. For a time he was remembered. And then as his contemporaries likewise were
gathered to the shades, the memory faded, and then there
was left of all of what he called 'the battle of his life'
a few verses, a few books, and that mute tablet in Worcester Cathedral.

He was, of course, a minor figure of his day: no more.
And in any event his tale has been told already.[1] His
relevance to this particular narrative lies in the area of
the effect he had upon many people of all sorts and conditions which was clearly of a highly unusual nature.
Some men impress by their abilities; some by wealth and
power, some by achievement: some yet again by their
obvious virtues: kindness, generosity, high-mindedness
and the like. Yet this Irish priest, it seemed, moved people
in quite a different way. He reminded them of someone.
He made Christ seem very near and real, personally
involved with them in their lives, precisely because he was

[1] William Purcell, *Woodbine Willie. A Biography*. Hodder & Stoughton.

himself so involved with the same Christ. The fact
manifested itself in many ways—strange evidences of a
relationship very exciting to discover because they
testified so strongly to the reality of the Lord whom this
man had met. So his compassions and his sorrows,
especially when aroused by human suffering, were of a
soul-shaking intensity. So were his angers with the
money-changers of contemporary society. He had, too, a
natural affinity with the poor and the dispossessed in its
nature a world away from the condescensions of the do-
gooder or the clinical attitudes of the professional social
worker. And, at the other end of the scale, intellectuals,
rather like that Nicodemus who came to Jesus by night,
often sought him out. Finally, at his death, he was worn
out and despairing, convinced that his life had been a
failure.

The echoes coming from it all were unmistakable,
and seemed to offer some explanation of the profound
effect of this man on so many of his contemporaries.
'He was the only person I ever met' one woman interviewed about her memory of him rather mysteriously said,
'who seemed in any way to make sense out of the tragedy
of men and women, and that was by his message of how
Christ was in everything with us, and we with him,
through death and beyond.' Another said 'he left a glow
behind him. I can't be more precise. It was just a glow;
a warm, reassuring sense not only that this life was not
all; but that it was in itself infinitely worth-while because
God was in it.' Yet another, who watched him, sometime
in the 'twenties, patiently enduring the jeers of a hostile
crowd, was much moved, and remembered the event for
many years. 'He taught by example as well as by precept.
He had the human touch, if ever a man had it; and bore

in his body the marks of the Lord Jesus. There was a world of sorrow in his deep eyes.'[1]

Now it is one of the consequences of studying closely, over a longish period of time, the records of one particular individual with a view to writing something about him, to get the feeling, after a while, that the man's very voice can be heard. He becomes a familiar. In this instance, when Geoffrey Studdert Kennedy, he whose name had reached out of obscurity by means of that memorial tablet in Worcester Cathedral, was thus the subject of a study, the effect was profound. Here was a meeting with one who, beyond question, had walked closely with Christ. The experience was both inspiring and encouraging: inspiring because the reality of his Christian witness was as clear as the results were dynamic. Here was a life, in fact, in which the practice of a faith, in one's own case too often a matter of duty only, became a blazing adventure in love and service. And it was encouraging because so many of the difficulties one had oneself met with and kept secret were openly acknowledged. Of these, doubt was the chief.

This, beyond all else, was where this meeting with Studdert Kennedy was so helpful. 'I have stood,' he used to say, 'in the last ditch many a time, and will again, before I die.' By that he meant that he had often had to face the possibility that the Christ whom he had pledged himself to follow was the product of human imagination. 'His sole concern was with the facts as they are, and against them he sought no protection' yet another admirer said of him. That such a man, utterly honest with himself, and under no illusions as to what the world was, should

[1] Ibid.

yet have found it possible to find in Christ a leader to be
followed all the way, to find him mirrored, indeed, in so
much of life, was a profound encouragement, as also was
the fact that he found the Church and its ministry of
word and sacrament so essential a factor in the mediating
of God to man. And if he could so gallantly overcome his
doubts, then here at least was warrant for the effort to
overcome one's own, and try to see faith, as he did, not
as a matter of certainties (the only certainties are dead
certainties); but as a constant adventure and a pledging
of oneself.

And besides this honest facing of doubt, and many a
sorrow, there was much humour in this man who thus
seemed to speak, although he were dead, of how excellent
a way it was with constancy to follow the master. He
was also highly intelligent; had something to say to life
as it was; a message for his day.

But, far beyond all else in importance was the fact that
he testified in himself to the reality of the Christ encounter.
Beyond a doubt, this is what so moved so many of those
who met him. Beyond a doubt, the same sense of power
exceeding what would otherwise have been his normal
capacity was discernible in him. More than a gifted, or
interesting a personality, his was a Christ-centred one.
And just because of that he helped many to believe,
including this present writer, who became his biographer.

Of course, there have been others. But it is important
to be quite clear as to the area in which these people have
been of such help. Most of us, looking back over life, can
recall with gratitude some who have meant much to us in
various capacities. There have been those who have
helped us by their love, others by their brains or special
skills; others by their generosity; others yet again, maybe,

by their criticisms. Their faces come up out of the years;
here a teacher, there, maybe, a colleague or a friend.
Even the exercise of thus recalling them is salutary as a
reminder of how little, how very little, we are self-sufficient, and how greatly we are dependent on the goodwill
of others. Yet those who have for us been notable as
the transmitters of a message, as it were, from the Lord
himself, just because he has been so clearly present in
them, are a class apart, What they have to give needs to
be measured by valuations different from those current
in the material world. It follows that they do not need
necessarily to be clever, or able, or powerful, or skilful
in some particular direction, or even to be of similar
cultural backgrounds, or to be conformers to the same
behaviour-pattern as ourselves in order that their particular kind of light—'the light that never was on land or
sea'—may shine upon us. They need only to have had
the great, if costly, blessing of being known to Christ,
and used by him. Most of the people encountered by this
present writer in the course of making the television
programmes referred to earlier in this book were of that
order. A few of them may be mentioned in fuller detail
at this point, not because they were the only persons of this
sort ever met with—far from it—but because they were
encountered in the course of that enterprise in an unusually concentrated form.

One of them was a woman in her late thirties, called
Phyllis Webber. Here was a rare soul indeed. She is dead
now. Yet, like Studdert Kennedy, she seems still to
speak. Hers was very largely a hidden life, lived entirely
in an invalid chair, she having been born with a spinal
affliction. She was discovered in the little town of Belper,
in Derbyshire, and a plate on the door of the tall stone

D

house in which she lived with her parents, said, 'Derby-shire School of Speech and Drama.' She was the Prin-cipal, a bare fact which concealed the far more striking circumstance that here was a severely handicapped person, who, far from being the recipient of sympathy herself was instead one who gave aid and comfort to others. Several of her pupils—they could with more accuracy have been called patients—were disturbed personalities who had been sent to her by their doctors. Under her guidance, they were led into harmony of mind through self-expression and contact with beauty in verse and word. Such was the theory. But the observer was left with the overpowering impression that they were led into wholeness of mind and spirit chiefly through contact with Phyllis Webber. One was reminded very much, seeing her in action one winter evening, of a passage in Mark's gospel: 'That evening after sunset they brought to him all who were ill or possessed by devils.' A Catholic priest in Eire, Father O'Flynn, of Cork, was about that time doing much the same kind of thing with people in similar difficulties. Miss Webber wrote him, asking if he could explain something of the odd power which both he—she had seen him featured on television—and she herself seemed to be the channels. Wisely, he replied he did not know; but that it should be enough for them thankfully and humbly to use it.

One thing is plain—and it was impossible to be long in Phyllis Webber's company without realizing it—that the power which worked in and through her came upon her from without. There was nothing apparent in the quiet existence she perforce led, or in her personal story, which was one of determined advance out of what might have been self-pitying invalidism into a life of remarkable service, otherwise to account for the very memorable personality which was hers. It is a great pity that words are so inadequate to describe the repose, the love and the understanding, half humorous, half sad, which seemed to flow from that otherwise quite ordinary woman. To say one felt moved to believe, because no other explanation seemed to be adequate, that Christ through the Holy Spirit was in her seems about as near as one can get to the effect of her essential quality—or quiddity, to use a useful term of the Schoolmen. It would certainly be more in harmony with the atmosphere she created than to attempt to account for it in terms of psychological phenomena, much as a solemn music would be less an intrusion upon a sanctuary than a sound of hammering. But who shall say, or presume to try to say, what exactly her power was? One may as well try to describe the appearance of the wind, of which it is possible only to describe what it does. It moves the trees: it stirs the seas: it can roar, it can blow softly. So it is with the wind of that Spirit: so it was with this Phyllis Webber. That is why I was helped, as were so many others, by her.

Christ through the Holy Spirit enters, however, into the lives of all sorts and conditions of people and shows remarkably few signs of being at all interested in those differences of cultural background which loom, perhaps inevitably, so large with most of us.

Douglas Hyde, another of this group, whose conversion to Roman Catholicism from active membership of the Communist Party was a matter of some comment at the time it took place, was idealogically a long way in outlook and predilection from myself. It may therefore be a fair comment that any evaluation one may have felt moved to make regarding the motivation for the costly step which this man had obviously taken was uncoloured by prejudice, favourable or otherwise. The facts of the matter were that, compelled to make a close study of Christian claims as a means of defending himself from difficulties into which some of his hitherto inaccurate critical statements in the press about the Church of which, as a Marxist, he was necessarily an opponent, he had found himself instead drawn in the opposite direction. The event was unexpected. This thing happened. Like Agrippa, when Paul preached before him, he felt moved to say, as he pondered Christian doctrine and evidences, 'You think it will not take much to win me over and make a Christian of me.'[1] Yet in the event he was persuaded by the sight of a humble worshipper slipping into a London Church where he happened to be sat at the back, and kneeling to say her Rosary. So some obscure Irish girl was an instrument of God's purposes in this instance.

Lest the telling of such a tale seems to imply an acceptance of the unfortunate notion that Christianity and Communism are irreconcilable opposites, or that the former is the preserve of all virtue as the latter of evil, let it be at once said that no such conclusion is intended or such a view held. The use of the faith to underwrite any political attitude is in any event objectionable. The only point made here is that this meeting with Douglas Hyde was another of these experiences which was helpful to this writer in that, as with the case of Phyllis Webber, it seemed to present such striking evidence of a power entering a personality from outside, as an objective rather than a subjective reality, and enabling that personality to develop along unexpected lines towards truth.

[1] Acts 26. 28.

Another of this same group of people who seemed so memorably to show forth this quality was an odd, mountebank of an Anglican priest called Father Potter of Peckham. In his day, and chiefly in the area of the Old Kent Road, south of London's river, he had been well known. His concern had always lain with unfortunates in general, and boys in trouble in particular. But his speciality was humour. The first impression he gave, at a first meeting, in the sparse little community he had founded, was that the whole of his ministry had been one continuous joke. The same impression, incidentally, was made by the little books he had produced about the time of our meeting.[1] He had been a boxer; he had been, one gathered, for a brief and highly unsuccessful period, a private detective. And then, with much difficulty ordained, he had been sent to a church in the last stages of decrepitude, with derelicts camping-out in the parish room and an organ full of dust. The vicarage was a pub, also disused. Such a tale, and much else of which these were but minor details, could have been banal and foolish. But deeper things came peeping out: memories of his boys, some of them very touching, like the altar book in the chapel of the Community which had as a marker a disc of the type developed by one lad in past times in place of coins in slot machines, and which was kept there as a daily memento of them all. There was a diploma from some Dartmoor prisoners in gratitude for a mission he had once conducted in that place. There was a manger in the chapel which really had once been a stable, so that he whom Father Potter liked to call the

[1] *Father Potter of Peckham*, Hodder & Stoughton.
More Father Potter of Peckham, Hodder & Stoughton.

Babe of Bethlehem could all the more suitably be worshipped there. The place, like the mind of the man, was an untidy, humorous rag-bag. And yet all the time there was something else. Certainly there was an underlying sadness in him, like the reality behind the grotesque make-up of a clown. Here was a man, one felt, who, knowing much of life, had always found laughter a good answer to some of its sadnesses. But also there was another quality about him which struck a still deeper chord. He gave the impression of being holy, in the strict sense of set aside, dedicated to the purposes of God. He could have been a very ordinary little Cockney. He was in fact quite extraordinary. And he was an inspiration because, apart from showing God so clearly at work in one life, he also demonstrated that humour and holiness go well together, and that it is not necessary to be solemn in order to be a saint.

There were, of course, as has been indicated already, a good many more men and women, met with in the course of making these television programmes, who equally clearly, if in different ways, showed forth this same unique quality—for unique it is, having nothing to do with the values of this world, and being as far removed from ordinary goodness and decency, admirable as these qualities are, as great beauty is from mere comeliness. Perhaps the chief value of the exercise is that it accidentally demonstrated how many there were to be found, although it is not presented there as anything novel, so much as something true. We could probably all make a list of such encounters if we tried. This is a critically important matter to the whole attempt at keeping the faith and trying, as best one may, to live the Christian life, particularly so for all those who find the difficulties of belief in a living God so difficult in today's materialist climate of opinion. The possibility of encounter with Christ in the lives of other people has always existed. It is also an experience which it is possible to have without being aware of it, as the blind do not know when a light has been switched on, or the deaf when a music has sounded. But when the light is seen and the sound is heard they are, at any rate in this writer's experience, unmistakable.

.   .   .   .   .

The second of the writers of this book, thinking of those who have fashioned his own life in this way, recalls five people in particular. The first, well known in his day, was the Principal of Westcott House, B. K. Cunningham. Here was a man, gentle and humorous, whose sense of balance and spiritual maturity rubbed off the harsh edges of prejudice and partisanship, and whose acceptance of suffering taught others how small and unimportant were their own difficulties and disappointments. Here was a man who, rather than ever drawing attention to himself, exercised a great talent in revealing to others latent potentialities which had hitherto been hidden from them. He made the Christian life attractive through his own attractiveness. He made those in his charge deeply aware that what really mattered were integrity, humility and courtesy, and he did so by the fact that these were the shining marks of his own life. This was the great lesson learnt from Cunningham—the normality of the Christian life, and of how it perfectly co-existed with the wholesome and the balanced. Here, in this man, was a living example of how spiritual progress does not depend upon emotion, but upon normal day by day obedience to God, expressed in regular worship, prayer and meditation. 'The Professor,' as he was called, was very deaf, and this writer, recalling him, treasures the picture of this elderly man with one hand cupped behind his deaf aid and the other pushing forward his little microphone, the better to catch what was being said to him, with his humorous eyes and mouth and the gentle compassionate face. B. K. Cunningham taught the value of the ordinary and the every-day transmuted by contact with Christ, with that Christ who spent his own life among ordinary people, and who revealed the supernatural through the natural, the extraordinary through the ordinary.

Another key figure in this writer's experience, was the famous founder padre of Toc H, the Reverend Tubby Clayton, at the time of this encounter with him at the height of his powers and fame, exercising an almost world-wide ministry from his church of All Hallows, Barking-by-the-Tower in the City of London. He was short, he was dumpy, his face radiated good humour; he was a kind of Pickwick. But he drew men to himself by the depth of his affection and by the force of his convictions. Always, sooner or later—sometimes much later, because he never hurried—this man would introduce his friends to Christ. And the manner in which he managed to do this was not by preaching or even by direct challenge, so much as by introducing people to service, and through personal service to the salvation of their souls. Often he would say, 'Life is like a swimming bath—most men learn to swim, not by being thrown into the deep end, but by spending some time in the shallow end, and then moving step by step out of their depth into the profundities of the supernatural.' And so he would say, 'Start by giving service to others, before long you

will discover the need for outside help, and that help
Christ alone can give.'

His, then, was a valuable lesson, that Christ can often
be met in the face to face encounter with other men in
need.

Quite different was the impression made by two priests,
Father Algy Robertson of the Society of St. Francis,
and his curate, Father Geoffrey Curtis, later of the
Community of the Resurrection. At the time of the encounter these two were running the parish of St. Ives,
near Cambridge. Robertson was a frail figure, with
compassionate eyes and yet with great vitality and
enthusiasm. The other, Curtis, was a complete contrast,
being fresh from Oxford and from a life of aesthetic
hedonism in Paris. The background of neither had pre-
vented both from experiencing a deep conversion—an
experience which, in the case of these two men, led both
towards what might be called evangelical catholicism.
The particular lesson which they had to teach was,
therefore, that of the value of spiritual disciplines, which
might be described, perhaps, as the military element in
the Christian life—the element of discipline and obedience
without asking questions. It was in the tradition of these
men that such things as confession, meditation, regular
and stated times of prayer, loomed large. Here was
encountered for the first time, the impressive and ancient
edifice of catholic piety and devotion. The impression
made by it was very great and has lasted.

But the tenderest and the most sacred of all these
memories is that of an obscure little man whose influence
persists for the one reason that he was the living embodi-
ment of that rarest of all qualities—holiness. This was
Father William of Glasshampton. The first meeting with

D*

this Anglican saint followed a journey from London into
the depths of the Worcestershire countryside, then a bus
ride to a bridge, then a walk of one and a half miles along
a path which finally petered out in a field. On the far
side of the field, leaning over a gate, was a small figure
in a black cassock, with a smiling face and penetrating
eyes. He wore a black skull cap and, by way of greeting,
slowly moved this little cap around his head, scratched
his beard, and said with an unforgettable smile 'Welcome
to Glasshampton.' This was the place where he had
retired from the world, to build up a small community
there. Through a gate was a garden smelling of flowers.
Inside was peace, and the cleanliness of those white-
washed walls, and the quiet of the place, together with an
indefinable atmosphere of something at once secret and
immensely holy, has left an abiding impression. This was
not only the first introduction to a friendship which lasted
for the whole of Father William's life; it was also an
introduction to the meaning of holiness—a quality which
attracted and intrigued, like a mysterious perfume. It was
a quality compounded, as was discovered as the man
and his disciplined life became better known, of gaiety,
iron determination, implicit obedience and costly personal
sacrifice. He had lived even then for many years under
the rule of poverty, chastity and obedience. From that
he had gone forward into the life of the solitary. And in
this courageous, lonely life of prayer and fasting he was,
in an extraordinary way in that day and age, influencing
for good the whole Church, setting a pattern of holiness
for many to see even if, as was the case with the writer of
these words, they were unable to follow.

He had, of course, his eccentricities. And yet even these
were holy eccentricities. One evening during that first

visit Father William was asked if, after the last Office of
the day, he would speak to the young men who had come
to see him. He said, 'I will, but only if the Lord gives me
something to say.' There was a long, long wait in silence
in the tiny chapel. There was no sound. Fifteen minutes
passed, and those who were present began to think that
Father William had fallen asleep. But suddenly he began
to speak, and his speech brought a tingle to the flesh.
For here was the voice, as it might have been, of such an
one as the author of the Fourth Gospel, steeped in holiness
and inner vision. Quietly, simply, Father William began
to speak of the love of God—that was all, but that was
much. Those who half an hour later left the chapel felt
almost as though they had touched the hem of the garment
of Christ himself. Father William seldom left his solitary
retreat at Glasshampton. But when he did, the impact
of his life was prodigious. It was as though he spoke and
moved with an authority wholly other from those of the
world, for there moved through him, quite clearly and
unmistakably, a power which was not his own.

A holy life, then, is like very precious ointment. Its
perfume is all-pervading; but its preparation is costly
and lengthy. Those who had the privilege of meeting
this holy man will never be quite the same again. Nor
will they forget the lessons which he so quietly taught:
that holiness is the greatest of all the Christian qualities;
but that it is not a matter of rules and forms and cere-
monies—though a rule of life, rigidly adhered to, as was
the case with him, is its backbone. Rather are holiness
and sanctity a loving response to the love of Christ, a
loving desire to go the extra mile, to turn the other
cheek, to pay the extra price, to make the double sacrifice.
Holiness is something which has rubbed off from the

personality of Christ himself on to that of some one or other of his creatures, such as Father William of Glasshampton, whom he chooses to honour in this way.

All these people, then, in their strikingly varied manners, and through strikingly varied qualities, have helped us. And what they have helped us in is to see that Christ may be met in and through people.

6. Objections

IN ALL these people, then, as in others in varying degrees
and manners, it has seemed to us that the spirit of Christ
has been so markedly manifest as to make it possible to say
that in them he has been met with. In the context of this
little book, as in far wider contexts, this is important
indeed, inasmuch as our purpose is to testify to the possibility and to the reality of such an encounter, as well as
to declare our beliefs that without it the maintenance of
a Christian faith professing life, hope, and meaning would
be impossible. Furthermore, this matter of a personal
Christ, that is to say, one who enters into individual lives
with a message for each life, and with a love for each life,
sometimes recognized, sometimes not, is equally critical
to those to whom, as we have stated, this book is particularly addressed—those who find nowadays a faith
professing life, hope and meaning difficult to maintain
or to receive. For both, the person of Christ personally
encountered is an essential. This is not new. Christianity
has never been a faith entered upon in the first place
through the possession of any particular body of knowledge, or through adherence to any particular body of
rules. It has been, as it still is, a religion of a person,
and that person Christ himself. It has always been,
therefore, very much in the tradition of those inarticulate
believers whom we were thinking of in the first chapter
of this book, that their faith has been markedly christocentric. And not the least of the 'earthborn clouds' there
referred to—elements in today's climate of opinion which

some of them, together indeed with many others, find, rightly or wrongly, inimical to belief, is the apparent removal from it, in some contemporary thinking, of this element of the personal relationship with a personal Christ who knows each of us and wills that we should know him.

Even so, it is important to take note of the objections which undoubtedly exist to this whole approach, the more so as such objections are upheld by some present-day Christians the quality of whose minds and the high purpose of whose thinking, especially as they are concerned with the re-shaping of the faith for a new age, are beyond question.

Basically, the objections would appear to be five in number. The first is that the whole approach is far too self-centred and, as such, is an aspect of that cult of the individual which has been such a feature of western society for so long. Love in the depths, love in community, a self-forgetting outreach into humanity as a response to the self-givingness of Christ would, it is maintained by up-holders of this objection, be an approach far more fitting to the needs of man today than such self obsession as represented, for instance, by Toplady's famous lines:

> 'Rock of Ages, cleft for *me*
> Let me hide *myself* in thee.'[1]

The second objection is that the emphasis of this highly personalized Christianity with its insistence on man's fallen state and his need to be saved or redeemed from it, may be faulted by being an appeal to man in his weakness rather than in his strength.

[1] Author's italics.

Thirdly, it is held that such an emphasis shows an indifference to sociological factors, exalting the individual at the expense of man collectively in society, and ignoring those influences upon him, such as arise, for instance, from the pressures of an industrial society, which, because they have more relevance to his life than anything else, must be the areas in which God's concern for him needs primarily to be demonstrated. The situation is sharply defined by Horst Symanowski in *The Christian Witness in an Industrial Society*:

For the church-estranged man there exists no connection between the world of his work and the church. . . . God . . . belongs to the religious realm: he has nothing to do with the everyday world, with work and with wages. Indeed, the machines run just as well without God's help . . . how can we make it clear to the church-estranged man that since Jesus Christ there simply is no longer any separation between God and man? Nothing at all is accomplished here by theological talk. The preaching of Jesus Christ would have to become flesh once again here and now in the world of work. . . .[1]

The fourth objection may be briefly stated—that personal response, in terms of self-surrender, to the claims of Christ, involves a degree of certitude and commitment which some now find both intellectually unwarranted, and psychologically undesirable in view of the closed mind to which it is held to give rise.

The fifth and last objection is that this insistence upon the uniqueness of Christ is unnecessarily exclusive of those many people of good will in the modern world who, every bit as much as the average Christian and a good deal

[1] Horst Symanowski, *The Christian Witness in an Industrial Society*, Collins.

more so than some, hunger and thirst after righteousness
but do not accept the primacy, or even the necessity, of
Christ. This position was powerfully represented by an
article in a Birmingham paper following a broadcast by
Doctor Billy Graham during his most recent Crusade in
Britain. To all the difficulties of modern man, the writer
alleged Doctor Graham had said, there was only one
answer: 'Belief in the one true God and His Son, Jesus
Christ, who sacrificed Himself for us.' The writer found
this selective, superficial, grossly inaccurate. He found it
particularly offensive in that it presented the world as
divided between the committed Christian on the one hand
and the materialistic, the unhappy, the unbalanced on the
other. It omitted what the writer called the 'middle
group'—people who by none of the conventional classi-
fications can be called Christians, yet who are living what
by ethical standards could fairly be called Christian
lives. 'In what is left of the twentieth century,' he concluded, 'the task of the Church is to become an open
society rather than a closed one, to let faith flow as it will,
and to concentrate on being a focus for the activities of all
who hold a Christian ethic in common. In this context
belief and unbelief can co-exist.' Predictably, he quoted
the Bishop of Woolwich in *Honest to God*: 'Among one's
intelligent non-Christian friends one discovers many who
are far nearer to the Kingdom of Heaven than they
themselves can credit. For while they imagine that they
have rejected the Gospel, they have in fact largely been
put off by a particular way of thinking about the world
which quite legitimately they find incredible.'[1] In so far,
therefore, as any insistence upon the importance of a

[1] *Birmingham Post*, June 20th, 1966.

personal encounter with Christ may be found to be exclusive of such people as this, then it is to be avoided.

Such objections are weighty. As to the first, the charge of self-centredness, it may be at once admitted that there have been, as no doubt there still are, many instances in which the Gospel has been understood in too narrowly personal terms. One of the chief dangers of the so-called spiritual life has always been that it could lead to exclusiveness and self-satisfaction, disfigurements which have marred the face of Christianity in many ages, including this one. Yet the truth is that in all ages Christ has called men, and called them, what is more, individually, as persons, never as members of any particular category or group. This 'person to person' element is inescapable and reaches far back to that Old Testament God who spoke with Moses as a man speaks with his friend, and to a vision of whom Isaiah, in another age and place, responded with the cry: 'Here am *I*; send *me*.' And later, across the centuries, Christ called Peter, Andrew, James and John as individuals by the lakeside as persons, rather than as members of a Galilean fishing collective! But the call of Christ has always been to action. That is the great point. He has summoned individuals to his service, often to their profound astonishment. He has chosen them: he has changed them. But always he has sent them out into the world to work for him. The charge of individualism can lie against this understanding of the Gospel only when that last stage is seen to be absent, and when a self-centred concern for the soul takes the place of what should be an outgoing love and service of mankind. The call of Christ, in fact, to the individual is not an end, but a beginning. But that the call must be there, and the personal response follow, is surely as true now as ever it was.

A good test of its genuineness is to ask a simple question 'What happened next?' 'What followed the call?' If no deepening of understanding or compassion ensued, or if no enriching of human experience took place, it may fairly be assumed that the call fell on deaf ears. But always it is to ourselves that the question should rightly be addressed. One result of a frank attempt to answer it is likely to be a renewed understanding of how necessary the call is in the first place, and how it must begin with a call to us by name, as individuals. 'I am the good shepherd: I know my own sheep and my sheep know me.'

What, then, of the objection that this personalized Gospel is an appeal to man in his weakness rather than in his strength? That man is insufficient of himself; and that he needs reconciliation with God through Christ in order that his broken relationship with God may be restored, has been of the essence of the Gospel from the beginning. The unhappily named conception of original sin—the notion, surely demonstrable from human behaviour at least as much in this terrible century as in any other—that human nature is biased towards the evil rather than the good, looms in the background here. And while it is the case that it has sometimes been interpreted in ways which many Christians find no longer acceptable, the general principle expressed by it continues to offer a sombrely impressive explanation of otherwise baffling phenomena in the human scene today. It ill becomes a century which has to include among its achievements the extermination camp and the thermonuclear weapon to accept too uncritically and, as is so often done, out of context, the phrase used by Dietrich Bonhoeffer in *Letters and Papers from Prison* 'man come of age,'[1] and therefore able to stand clear, if he so wishes, of that dependence upon God which over-arched the thinking of his forebears. If man's moral and spiritual development had kept pace, or even shown any signs of doing so, with his undoubtedly increased mastery of his physical environment, then the picture might be very different. Unfortunately, it is not so, and the notion continues to be alarming of today's, and even more of tomorrow's, man working to the assumption that he is indeed self-sufficient, that he can build his world without God, and that his ills are curable solely on psychological or economic lines. Nor is it so only for what it may portend for his ultimate fate. It is daunting also as regards his accessibility, or rather non-accessibility, to what continues to be an essential part of the Gospel—the proclamation of man's need and of Christ's unique power to meet it.

Of course, part of the objection to this appeal to man in his weakness lies in a realization of the fact that the areas of his weakness are, it is often claimed, diminishing. His fears, his inadequacies, even his follies, may before long be so treatable by his own unaided resources especially psychological and technological as to render any

---

[1] The actual passage is: 'There is no longer any need for God as a working hypothesis, whether in morals, politics or science. Nor is there any need for such a God in religion or philosophy. . . . So our coming of age forces us to a true recognition of our situation *vis-à-vis* God. God is teaching us that we must live as men who can get along very well without him. . . .'

Elsewhere, in notes of a book he would like to have written, he lists among its topics: 'The decay of religion in a world that has come of age. God is a working hypothesis, as a stop-gap for our embarrassments.'

Letter and Papers from Prison, pp. 122 and 164, Fontana Books, Collins. A further corrective to taking such passages as this out of context may be had by a reading of Bonhoeffer's *Christology*, Collins, 1966, when his deep personal piety is shiningly evident. His last act, before his martyr's death at the hands of the Gestapo, was to conduct a service.

appeal to a power 'outside' himself anachronistic. But is this really so? As an argument it would carry more weight if the human scene were less perilous and tragic than in fact it is. Self-sufficient man, considering himself the master of things, is a terrifying portent. Paul, as usual, seems to have something to say here: 'Make no mistake about this: if there is any one among you who fancies himself wise—wise, I mean, by the standards of this passing age—he must become a fool again to gain true wisdom. For the wisdom of this world is folly in God's sight.'[1]

Time and again it has been to men and women in their weakness that Christ has most movingly and fruitfully spoken. Christian experience is rich in instances of how the need for Christ has had to be felt before the discovery of him has been possible. The hard fact is that men and women in their strength, riding high on the tides of fortune, are not likely to feel such a need and therefore unlikely to make such a discovery. It is, on the contrary, and on the record, in times of dereliction, of sorrow, of humiliation, of need, sickness or any other adversity, that the voice of God, always a still, small one, is most likely to be heard. '*Out of the depths* have I cried unto thee, O Lord: Lord hear my voice.' The cry of the psalmist still echoes. So does another voice: 'Come to me all whose work is hard, whose load is heavy: and I will give you relief.' If that is a comfortable word to man in his weakness, then at least it is an august one, and many there are who have heard it gladly.

Certainly, to seek to speak exclusively of God to man in his weakness, and to emphasize his sinfulness while appearing to take little account of his strength, is to run

[1] 1 Corinthians 3. 18-19.

the risk of excluding God from those areas of achievement; scientific, artistic, technical, which mean so much to
man in the modern world. But to suppose that man
should be spoken to only in his strength is surely to ignore
not only ineradicable facts about human nature; but also
elements in the Gospel which are unalterably there,
whether we approve of them or not.

We come now to the third of these objections—that
undue emphasis upon personal sinfulness, and upon
personal encounter with Christ as a way of liberation,
ignores those sociological factors in a man's life which
operate powerfully, whether he knows it or not, in making
him what he is. There is a formidable degree of truth in
this. The degree to which the churches have often been
both indifferent to the political and economic facts of life
as well as unduly wrapped up in their own inward-
looking concerns, has been a dark chapter in their history.
It has shown failures in awareness and compassion wholly
culpable, never more so than in the long years which
saw the growth of industrialism. The indifference to,
or ignorance of, the social and economic conditions of
their time shown by the Tractarians, to take one instance
alone, is very remarkable. The proportion of time and
energy given by the Church in general in the nineteenth
century to matters of social justice, was infinitesimal
compared to the time and energy given, as is acknowledged in a later chapter of this book, to questions of
theology, doctrine, and church order. The damage thus
inflicted not only upon the victims of this indifference, but
upon the churches themselves, has, of course, been
enormous. The gulf of mutual incomprehensibility which
now separates the great bulk of the working population

from the Church—a gulf which may well take generations
to bridge—may indeed be said to have been created at
this point. The bland acceptance of such scars upon the
face of society as poverty and class distinction, existing
side by side with protestations of Christian profession,
has been a feature of much Christian history which can
only be described as extraordinary. But things are
different now, and those of our Christian forebears who
sowed this particular wind have left to us who follow
them the reaping of the whirlwind. The writer of the
Birmingham Post article already quoted has this to say on
this point:

'We are now more Christian than at any time in our history.
Goodness knows, there is still a lot that is wrong, and is going
wrong; but to have exchanged the Victorian parade of piety
for the positive concern now shown for the under-dog is a
good bargain, so far as I am concerned. . . . It is true that
we no longer accept misery and destitution as a natural
concomitant of the station in life to which a man has been
called; and the fact that this development should have taken
place in what is commonly called a secular society is something
that ought to give Christians pause for thought.'

Indeed it should. And yet, even when all that has been
acknowledged, it remains true that the Christian record
of social service, invariably at its richest based upon an
uninhibited preaching of Christ, has been a splendid one.
And this needs to be said, if only in common justice.
It is being far too often overlooked, perhaps especially by
those who, in an ardent desire to get alongside those who
cannot accept their own Christian presuppositions, seem
only too anxious to play down the enormous achievements
of the tradition in which they themselves stand. Christians

OBJECTIONS 113

have, as a fact, a singularly large inheritance of the tradition of good works. Whether these represented an outpouring of energy and love which would have been better
directed into channels of political action rather than of
ambulance work, as some would maintain, may be a
matter for debate. If, however, some of the many human
casualties, the poor, the outcast, the oppressed, the
miserable and the under-privileged—that scarecrow army
of yesterday's industrialism—would be more likely,
could they be summoned back, to rise up and call blessed
those who discussed their predicament rather than those
who did something in the name of Christ about it, is
open to question. Let it never be forgotten that the social
services of today, including educational and medical
services, are to a large extent following where Christian
pioneers made the first halting footsteps. Christian do-
gooders have been the shapers of social history. Indeed,
they have been the redeemers of it. The social consequences of the Industrial Revolution were brutal and
sombre in the extreme. To what pitch of degradation
the onward rush of the industrial machine would eventually have reduced society, without the ameliorating
influence of Christian charity manifested in countless
ways, is a sombre thought. The Church has every reason
to glory in its record in this respect. Time and again it
has been Christian people carrying a light in dark places
who have made it possible for the under-privileged to
regain hope.

The social history of the churches abounds in great
names of those who fought for the rights of humanity,
and fought for them—which is the point here—in the
name of Christ and in the power of Christ. The Franciscans
in the stinking alleys of mediaeval towns: the Methodists

proclaiming the Gospel under the very shadow of the mill: the Evangelicals with their immense practical concern for the poor—a concern marvellously shown in Kathleen Heasman's book *Evangelicals in Action.*[1] These were but some among many other names which easily spring to mind: Wesley, Booth, Barnardo, William Temple with his passion for social justice, Basil Jellicoe among the slums of St. Pancras. The mass of Christian action of all kinds in many ages has led to the amassing of a record of practical benevolence which has never been equalled, and indeed never been approached, by any other faith. And underpinning all this has always been the offer of the Gospel, and a personal response to the love of Christ in the individual life. However, other times, other manners. Those who wish to make that love of Christ impinge upon society as we know it now may well turn to other ways of doing so. But whether any ways will be found to be ultimately fruitful which leave him as a person out of it, which avoid or regard as out of date any emphasis upon personal experience of him, is at least open to question.

'Is God alive or is he dead?' asked an article in the *Sunday Times* recently.

'Christians today are being invited by rival camps of theologians to look again at the central concern of their belief in God. The "God is dead" men argue that the Church has muffed its preaching about God and that most of us are away back in the Old Testament with a God who is quite properly dead, and that we have not yet begun to know the living God who is Jesus. This Jesus is present in every human hand and face, and wherever there is energy, life and change. This world can never be Godless, they say, for this Jesus who is

[1] *Evangelicals in Action*, Bles.

God is a living process of vital life which is flooding the created world. They see God everywhere and in everything. He is a secular God which the Church finds it hard to recognize. This social gospel, as it is sometimes called, is suspect by many because it seems to go along with the world, and is using the worldly language instead of religious language to express its meaning.'

True enough; a wholehearted identification with the concerns of the world necessarily follows from an adequate view of the Incarnation, which sees God in his world everywhere, and not as the pale captive of this or that ecclesiastical interest. But those to whom personal experience of a personal Christ is of the essence of the faith which they try, however humbly, to live out, must preserve for themselves a right to say that history so far affords no instance of fruitful Christian action serving the world in its day and generation, which has left out of account, or which has regarded as non-essential, this vital element.

The fourth objection to this whole approach is that personal response to the claims of Christ involves a degree of certitude no longer intellectually warranted, and a degree of commitment no longer psychologically desirable. Certainly, any faith based upon the Bible as an infallible book or upon the Church as an infallible body, is no longer tenable. It is a long time now since various Samsons pulled down those twin pillars of former certitudes. And if, in the process, much ecclesiastical bric-à-brac, to use an admirable phrase of Miss Monica Furlong's, has been got rid of, who can not but rejoice? Yet what we are left with, as has so often happened and as no doubt will happen again, is Jesus, and him only. Long before elaborate doctrinal statements were formulated, the early

Church had lived by subscription to the simple proposition that 'Jesus is Lord.' Given that certitude we can surely learn to live without many others, and can be prepared, by its light, to follow the trail of the truth wherever it leads us. But commitment is surely vital. There can be no half measures about this. 'He who is not for me is against me,' is as true now as ever it was. Commitment involves recognition of all the consequences flowing from acceptance of the proposition that Jesus is indeed Lord, and this in its turn involves a continuous effort to subjugate our will to his, and to recognize in him a power and a personality wholly other and outside ourselves. If this is to talk religious language, as some would object, seeing in it one of those barriers to fruitful dialogue with the world, then so be it. The fact remains—and it is a fact—that time and again it has been shown that commitment attracts and does not repel, and that those prepared uninhibitedly to witness to their Christian commitment have often more to give to the world of their day —a world in which there are usually very many men and women searching for this very quality—than those without it. 'The sole purpose of having an open mind,' William Temple once said, 'is in order that eventually we may close it on something.' What better point than on the statement that 'Jesus is Lord' and on the commitment which follows therefrom?

Is this—and here we come to the fifth and last of these objections—necessarily something which must be divisive as between Christian and non-Christian? It need not be so, nor in fact has it proved to be. The notion that the Gospel must be secularized in order that Christian dialogue with the non-Christian world may be fruitful is relatively new. Nor, in terms of that dialogue, does it seem to work very well. It became clear, in the course of the *Honest to God* debate of a few years ago, that some agnostics and humanists were understandably incensed at being assured that there was in fact far less distance than they imagined between their position and that of the Christian. There *is* a difference; and this difference comes at the point, as they would be the first to acknowledge, of personal commitment to Christ. That it is a position to be held with humility is true; but that it should be held with definiteness and without qualification would seem to be, not only the plain duty of the Christian, but also often the wish of those who, for honourable reasons, find themselves unable personally to subscribe to it.

This has been a long digression. But it has seemed necessary, in order that some of these current objections to a highly personalized faith which has meant so much to the passing generations, and continues to mean much to many now, may be fairly examined. Perhaps one of the great virtues of the current debate as to the forms and manner and justifiable assertions of contemporary Christianity is that it encourages people to take a hard look at what they really do believe. For our part, then, we believe in the Christ who comes to us as a person in age after age, and who, moving out from the intimacies of private lives, impinges with power through them upon their day. His instrument of so doing is the Holy Spirit. What is this Holy Spirit? How does it operate in and through the individual? Let us think together about this.

7. The Holy Spirit and the Individual

THERE ARE two things which it seems necessary to say before we come to this thinking together about the Holy Spirit. The first is to re-state, at this point, the purpose of this book. It is to pass on, from two very ordinary men, something of hope and encouragement to those many who have felt themselves blown off course by those winds of change which are now affecting the whole Christian scene. The only reason, let it at once be said, why they feel able to speak at all in terms of hope and encouragement, is that the more they think upon these things, the more they feel hope and encouragement to be possible.

One of the reasons for both is the recurrent marvel, as mysterious as incalculable, of the impingement of the Holy Spirit upon the human scene. It has happened before that, when the tide of faith seems to have receded very far, leaving depressing expanses of the mud flats of disillusion visible under grey skies, that the tide has come in again on a wind of the Spirit. Though the forms which faith assumes thereafter have, again often, been different from those to which some had been accustomed, yet that the tide did come in again and that hearts were brave again and arms were strong, is a fact of history.[1]

[1] The process can be seen, for instance, very clearly in Professor A. G. Dicken's *The English Reformation* (Batsford, 1964) where the contrast between the forms and manners of late mediaeval religion as described in the first chapter can be seen to be remarkably different from those of post-Reformation Christianity. People who lived through the decline and fall of the former might well have been forgiven if, as some did, they imagined this to be the end of all things. But they would have been wrong.

Secondly, it seems necessary, before speaking of this Holy Spirit in the life of the individual, to say what we mean by this term 'the Holy Spirit'—a term too often used too loosely. What, then do we mean?

'The primitive and fundamental idea of "spirit" in the Old Testament is that of active power or energy, power superhuman, mysterious, illusive, of which the ruach or wind of the desert was not so much the symbol as the most familiar example.

'When we read books of travel in Arabia, such as Doughty's *Arabia Deserta*, we are often made to feel the overwhelming power of the wind across the desert, scorching heat by day and piercing cold by night. This elemental force, incalculable and irresistable and invisible, was surely akin to that which could shape a man's behaviour as strangely as the desert sand was shaped before the blast.'[1]

It was a force which came upon men from outside themselves, and the Old Testament abounds in examples of it. It is this ruach, or wild energy, which rushes upon Samson when he slays a lion or man, or breaks the ropes that bind him. It is this ruach, this inspiring force, which comes upon David after his anointing by Samuel: 'Then Samuel took the horn of oil, and anointed him in the midst of his brethren: and the Spirit of the Lord came mightily upon David from that day forward.'[2] Pharaoh had the same quality in mind when he said of Joseph 'Can we find such a one as this, a man in whom the Spirit of God is?'[3] The word and the concept have an enormous

[1] H. Wheeler Robinson, *The Christian Experience of the Holy Spirit*, Fontana Books.
[2] 1 Samuel 16. 13.   [3] Genesis 41. 38.

history, coming to imply an essential quality of energy and power, closely identified with the nature of God.

> Cast me not away from thy face,
> And take not thy Holy Spirit (ruach) from me

says Psalm 51, and the 139th, that song to the omnipresence and inescapability of God, asks:

> Whither shall I go from thy spirit (ruach)?
> Or whither shall I flee from thy face?

The sense of daemonic power and excitement in this concept of spirit as power and energy coming from without, inexplicable and irresistible, is caught in Shelley's 'Ode to the West Wind':

> O wild West Wind, thou breath of Autumn's being,
> Thou, from whose unseen presence the leaves dead
> Are driven, like ghosts from an enchanter fleeing,
> Yellow, and black, and pale, and hectic red,
> Pestilence-stricken multitudes: O thou,
> Who chariotest to their dark wintry bed
> The winged seeds, where they lie cold and low,
> Each like a corpse within its grave, until
> Thine azure sister of the spring shall blow
> Her clarion o'er the dreaming earth, and fill
> (Driving sweet buds like flocks to feed in air)
> With living hues and odours plain and hill:
> Wild Spirit, which art moving everywhere;
> Destroyer and preserver; hear, oh, hear!

In the New Testament Spirit is one of the marks of the Kingdom, the new dispensation, the new way of life made possible in him, which Christ brought and preached. When, therefore, he bequeathed the Spirit to them, they were excitingly conscious of the long line of descent by

which this power came, winding as it did like a golden
thread in and out of the spiritual history of their people.
The difference was that now the Spirit came, not only
to the prophets and the seers, but upon all men and women,
however humble, who were able to say from the bottom
of their hearts, with unequivocal conviction, that 'Jesus
is Lord.'

'It is in the pages of the New Testament that we first
see the full significance of this long development. The
Christian consciousness might be not unfairly described
as a democratization of the prophetic consciousness
through the gift of the Holy Spirit . . . this consciousness
includes a new experience of God through Jesus Christ,
a new emphasis on the supernatural, a new sense of power,
notably in the conflict with those many "spiritual"
powers which thronged the air of the ancient world.
The conflict can be traced through the synoptics in the
war waged by Jesus in the power of the Spirit against
the demons of disease and insanity, or in the spirit world
of the Apostle Paul, filled with principalities and powers,
or again, in more etherealized form, in the Johannine
conception of the world, the flesh and the devil. The new
sense of power, always the characteristic creation of the
Spirit, breaks into consciousness at Pentecost, where it is
seen in the creation of a new fellowship.'[1]

This is the Spirit of Pentecost. This is the 'Spirit of
Truth' promised by Christ. 'I will ask the Father, and
he will give you another to be your Advocate, who will
be with you for ever—the Spirit of truth. The world
cannot receive him, because the world neither sees nor
knows him; but you know him, because he dwells with

[1] Ibid.

you and is in you.'[1] This is the Spirit who will come in
Christ's name, who will bear witness of God, who will be
sent by Christ from the Father, and whose coming will be
a consequence of Christ's going from the world. His work
will glorify Christ.

Such an outline, inevitably, does violence to the
complexity and profundity of the matter. What might be
called the trail of the Holy Spirit may indeed be followed
from that mysterious principle of creation which brooded
over the face of the waters in the first chapter of Genesis,
to the outpouring of the Spirit in New Testament
Christianity and beyond that, it may well be, to wherever
the divine principle of creation is in progress, whether it be
scientific or artistic. One thing is certain: this high
voltage, incalculable, amazing power is something far
greater than the mini-Spirit tamed and shrunken in the
Victorian hymn

> And his that gentle voice we hear,
> Soft as the breath of even,
> That checks each fault, that calms each fear,
> And speaks of Heaven.

Much nearer the stature of the true Holy Spirit is,
surely, the *Veni Creator*:

> Come, Holy Ghost, our souls inspire,
> And lighten with celestial fire;
> Thou the anointing Spirit art,
> Who dost thy seven-fold gifts impart.
>
> Thy blessed unction from above
> Is comfort, life, and fire of love;
> Enable with perpetual light
> The dullness of our blinded sight.

[1] John 14. 16-17.

What, then, of this Holy Spirit and the life of the individual? What does the Holy Spirit *do* to a man? It has been well said that the reality of any spiritual experience can be tested by the degree of change in the individual life to which it gives rise. On this test, then, there would seem to be at least four ways in which the Spirit acts in the life of the individual—manifestations which can be found occurring time and again in Christian experience. First, the Spirit brings vitality. The difference here is between existing and living. How many people exist, and how many live, in the sense of fully expressing their personalities in a cause and in a loyalty larger than themselves, would be an interesting question. It could be that our materialist, present-day way of life is singularly poor in this precious quality—a quality which tends to slip out of reach once the spirit-orientated view of life has faded. Be that as it may, vitality in this sense has been a characteristic mark of identity of the Holy Spirit in all ages. Perhaps it was this that lay behind the remark of Christ to Nicodemus, a highly intelligent and worthy citizen who yet lacked this very quality and was uneasily aware of it: ' "In truth, in very truth I tell you, unless a man has been born over again he cannot see the Kingdom of God." "But how is it possible," said Nicodemus, "for a man to be born when he is old? Can he enter his mother's womb a second time and be born?" Jesus answered, "In truth I tell you, no one can enter the Kingdom of God without being born from water and spirit. Flesh can give birth only to flesh; it is spirit that gives birth to spirit." '[1]

[1] John 3. 3-7.

E

The second manner in which the Spirit makes his presence unmistakably felt, lies in the area of the relationship between the individual and God. It is as though the Spirit-filled personality becomes aware not only of God, but of his own relation to him. It is an I/Thou relationship; one in which the person concerned becomes acutely aware of the responsibility which is his to respond —and much of the Christian life is in fact a response to an action of God—of the responsibility of using his time, his talents, his goods and his efforts, all that he has and is, in the service of God. Paul's phrase about being 'alive to God,' itself comes alive at this point. The new man in Christ, as he says in Romans, will respond to the new life which has become possible in him by dying to the old life which he knew before. 'In the same way you must regard yourselves as dead to sin and alive to God, in union with Christ Jesus'[1]

And thirdly, just because of this new awareness of his own personality *vis-à-vis* God, brought to birth by the Spirit, the individual becomes aware more acutely and with far greater reality and with sense of responsibility for them, of other people. That is to say, he is enabled to see other people as persons of significance and value because they are, in the eyes of God, of significance and value.

'The first postulate of Christian experience seems to be the reality, the dignity, the eternal value of human personality. This gives a cosmic setting to the humblest life; what more can be said of man's importance than that there is joy in the presence of the Angels of God over one sinner that repenteth?'[2]

[1] Romans 6. 10-11.
[2] H. Wheeler Robinson, *The Christian Experience of the Holy Spirit*, Fontana Books.

So the Spirit-filled person begins to see others in this new and precious light. For that matter, he begins to see everything in this new and precious light, so that the ordinary becomes transmuted into the extraordinary, and life itself becomes a rare and precious experience. 'I still remember walking down the Notting Hill main road and observing the extremely sordid landscape with joy and astonishment. Even the movement of the traffic had something universal and sublime about it.' So wrote Evelyn Underhill in one of her letters, and the passage aptly describes this new way of looking at things in the power of the Spirit. It is the same power which lay behind the world-transforming fellowship which emerged from the coming of the Spirit upon the Disciples at Pentecost and which has ever since, where the Christian life has been at its best, made creative fellowship a mark of that life. And here it may be added, that where in fact such fellowship is notably absent as, for instance, in the frigid self-enclosed, mutually rejecting attitude of some Christian congregations, the scandal is all the greater and the loss all the more grievous.

The fourth manifestation of the Holy Spirit is to be found in the desire for service, which itself is a manifestation of love in action, a quality which Paul places among the first of the fruit of the Spirit. This desire for service is the very opposite of keeping oneself to oneself. It is a development from coming alive to God, so that the individual becomes alive to other people, and desires to express a new-found sense of responsibility in practical outgoing service. Here again, Christian history is rich in instances of this very quality. Whether whatever of the faith we possess, or think we possess, is a veneer or the real thing may well be tested at this very point, as to how far we have been moved by the Spirit to this outgoing love for all his creation—a love which, in our practical-minded civilization, will find its most natural expression in the service of others.

Yet it is very easy at this point to fall into that very fault of excessive individualism which, as we saw, is one of the objections sometimes urged against this personalized understanding of the response to the claims of Christ. The caution is necessary, because it must never be forgotten that the Holy Spirit comes not so much to individuals as to individuals in community. This is where membership of the Church is of such critical importance. At Pentecost the Spirit was bequeathed to a group of individuals who had prepared themselves for his coming by prayer, the breaking of bread, the Apostles' doctrine and by team-work in which they shared all things in common. Then, and only then, was the Spirit able to weld them into a still deeper fellowship, and to send them out into the service of the world. Even so, we must never fall into the trap—and it is literally a trap because it holds us in one place—of supposing that the operation of the Spirit is confined to the life of the Church in the narrower meaning of the word. Indeed, it is sometimes only too evident that the Spirit is not in fact there operating, and we shall be suggesting a little later on that this may well be one of the main reasons why the Church, as many of us know it, has for the moment ceased to attract and to excite, and why many of those who are faithful, if inarticulate, members of it sometimes grow weary at the monotony of the path which their loyalty impels them to travel. Meanwhile, it is well to note that this dynamic and creative Spirit of God is at work in great art, in science, and indeed wherever human energy is used for the extension of knowledge and for the betterment of mankind. Most of us can easily, for that matter, call to mind people who are not the members of any church, but whose public spirit, love of their fellows expressed in social service and involvement in the life of society, we must humbly recognize. This has been well called the extra-mural work of the Holy Spirit—the 'outside the walls' activity of him who energizes and inspires 'all that is true, all that is noble, all that is just and pure, all that is lovable and gracious, whatever is excellent and admirable.'[1]

It was, then, encounter with the Holy Spirit which shaped New Testament Christianity and which made of it a power able ultimately to turn the world upside down. What surely we have to ask ourselves, therefore, is in what ways, if it be so, our own faith today is deficient in this life and power. By so doing we may well find a way out from that discouragement and disillusion which lies heavily upon both some Christians themselves today, and also upon those men and women of goodwill who look to them for a spiritual dynamic and do not find it.

The Spirit which descended upon the early Church brought, then, a new experience of God. God ceased to be remote, up there, over there, back there, in the gaps, and became one who was here, at the heart of life, discoverable in fellowship and in experience of prayer and worship and service. Secondly, through this new experience of God, men and women became more conscious of the supernatural world, the world of the spirit, where both good and evil mysteriously co-existed. On the side of the former, therefore, they felt themselves to be

[1] Philippians 4. 8.

continually involved in a struggle against the latter. As Paul put it: 'For our fight is not against human foes, but against cosmic powers, against the authorities and potentates of this dark world, against the supernatural forces of evil in the heavens.'[1] And then—and here we link up with what we were saying about the Holy Spirit and the life of the individual—these early Christians also became conscious of one another in a new and vigorous way, recognizing their mutual responsibilities. No longer did they ask: 'Am I my brother's keeper?' They knew they were. The problems of one were the responsibility of all. If there was a famine in Jerusalem, it was the concern of Christians far away in Corinth or in Ephesus, just as in the modern world poverty and over-crowding in Hong Kong should be the concern of Christians in a Surrey suburb or in New Jersey.

Experience of the Spirit brought also a new sense of deliverance from blind fate and blind chance. This is not the place to elaborate upon the superstitions of the ancient world in which the early Church had its birth, except to say that they were many, existing side by side, just as they do in the modern world. To have 'the liberty and splendour of the children of God,' to quote Paul in Romans again, was a notable liberation from them! Those who felt themselves guided by a loving, purposive God could feel themselves delivered from the bondage of fate. They knew who they were and where they were going.

Obviously this early Church had its share of the stupid, the obstinate, the psychologically mixed up, just as the modern Church has, human nature being what it is.

[1] Ephesians 6. 12.

But that it had this strange power moving in and through it is testified to by the magnitude of its achievements. Nothing is to be attained by exaggerating or idealizing the virtues of these early Christians; but it is a failure in historical impartiality to fail to recognize the splendour of their record. Equally it is a failure in truth and candour not to recognize that the Church today, and notably those parts of it which have become with the passage of time heavily institutionalized, compares ill with it in these respects. Of personal piety there is much—often far more than is often recognized, as we were saying in the first chapter of this book. But of these exciting and dynamic qualities which the Spirit, as the record testifies, brought to the early Church, there often seems little enough. Such a statement can perhaps best be substantiated by taking these gifts of the Spirit one by one as they were in fact manifested in the early Church and comparing the picture thus presented with the scene in the Church today.

There is certainly a lack of certitude. And yet to maintain, as some do, that this is one consequence of today's theological great debate is surely to be mistaken. The Holy Spirit which, as Christ promised, will lead us to all truth, is strong enough and resilient enough not to require the support of man-made, and therefore of time-vulnerable, so called certitudes. Christians who dislike being, as the phrase goes, 'disturbed in their faith' may well take note that to disturb and to arouse is, in fact, one of the characteristic activities of the Spirit. It is a great pity that Christianity, which began as a revolutionary faith, should have had its practice so often interpreted in terms of tranquillity, peace and composure. But where the Holy Spirit is truly present there comes a

certainty of faith amply strong enough both to adjust itself
to change, gladly and adventurously, and yet to feel that
God is always present, in and through all. If there is one
thing that is abundantly clear from the Book of the Acts
it is that the early Christians spoke with authority and
acted with conviction. This is a faith that overcomes the
world, and is the most precious gift of the Spirit. But the
current theological ferment is not only likely to continue
but should be welcomed as part of the exciting process of
pouring new wine into new bottles. Given the Spirit,
Christians should be able not only to take it; but to rejoice
in it. These things are not new. The theological ferments
of the first four or five centuries of the Church's life were
of an intensity and complexity to make those of today
seem mild indeed by comparison. Meanwhile, it may be
observed that the correlation, by so many contemporary
orthodox Christians, of unalterable certitudes with the
life of faith, may well be a sign not so much that the
Spirit is with them; but that the Spirit is notably absent!

Secondly, early Christianity was conscious of the
supernatural world and, as a consequence, was intensely
aware of the forces of good and evil emanating from that
world which involved them, as the allies of the former,
in a constant struggle. Few things can do, or in fact
have done, more to emasculate the faith, and to remove
from it the inspiriting tensions of conflict, than the notion
that this spiritual warfare is a thing of the past. Those
who would thus dismiss it, let it be remembered, have yet
to account for such appalling and inexplicable wellings-up
of evil as the extermination camp, the saturation raid on
open cities, and now the push-button mass murder made
possible by the nuclear weapon. We are living in the most
bloodstained century since the beginning of time. It is

difficult, to say the least of it, to account for all these phenomena in terms of rational thought, or to continue to maintain, as could a nineteenth-century rationalist, living in an age when these things were undreamt of, that reason would solve all. Rather does it begin once again to look as if these early Christians were right, and that we do indeed have a warfare on our hands against unseen powers of evil, against wickedness in high places. The Christian Church cannot, in any event, have it both ways, continuing to use the terminology of this conflict on the one hand while intellectually dismissing the possibility of it on the other. For our part, we would claim that this warfare is real, and that it is a mark of the Spirit to be aware of it. The New Testament is rich in the vocabulary of conflict, and of birth and death; putting off and putting on, of dying to sin and rising to new life. Paul unashamedly uses the metaphors of warfare. 'Put on all the armour which God provides, so that you may be able to stand firm against the devices of the Devil. For our fight is not against human foes, but against cosmic powers, against the authorities and potentates of this dark world, against the superhuman forces of evil in the heavens. Therefore, take up God's armour; then you will be able to stand your ground when things are at their worst, to complete every task and still to stand. Stand firm, I say. Buckle on the belt of truth; for coat of mail put on integrity; let the shoes on your feet be the gospel of peace to give you firm footing; and with all these, take up the great shield of faith, with which you will be able to quench all the flaming arrows of the Evil One. Take salvation for helmet; for sword, take that which the Spirit gives you— the words that come from God.'[1]

[1] Ephesians 6. 10-17.

F

And then, over against this dark world, there is the bright world which we cannot see or feel, but with the eye and with the touch of faith through the Spirit, and into which the poet and the artist can often lead us more confidently than any others. The denial of the reality of this world, for which the term supernatural may be used, is a grievous thing, and has done much to bleach out that colour from the practice of his religion which every man needs as a flower needs the sun. Yet it is still there, in spite of all our technologies.

Let a poet re-state it for us:

> O world invisible, we view thee,
> O world intangible, we touch thee,
> O world unknowable, we know thee,
> Inapprehensible, we clutch thee! . . .
>
> The Angels keep their ancient places;—
> Turn but a stone, and start a wing!
> 'Tis ye, 'tis your estranged faces,
> That miss the many-splendoured thing.[1]

Western man today is in danger of spiritual death from lack of exposure to this element of the supernatural. Materialism is its deadly enemy, just as it is the deadly enemy of true religion, a fact which has been known to the ancient cultures of the East for a long time. Lack of spirituality is also a danger to the Church and, in so far as it is frequently a quality notable nowadays for its absence, it may here again be noted that in this respect it is impoverished by comparison with the Spirit-filled early Church.

It is also true that, under the leading of the same Spirit, the early Church was able to transcend barriers of race,

---

[1] Francis Thompson, *The Kingdom of God.*

class and status. There indeed was a community in which all sorts and conditions of men and women could, and as a fact did, meet together on the level of an equality unattainable in the outer world.

When Paul could say, 'There is no question here of Greek and Jew, circumcised and uncircumcised, Barbarian, Scythian, freeman, slave; but Christ is all, and in all,'[1] he was stating the exact truth of many a little Christian community of that ancient world, over the entrance to whose meeting places there could with truth have been written 'abandon rank all ye who enter here.' The contrast with the modern Church, which has a long way indeed yet to go before it can overcome race and status prejudices, is striking indeed. Even so, it should in all justice be said that the Church is a good deal better than much of the world in this respect, as Christian leadership in matters of race equality bears witness. The point here is that these things are possible in the Spirit but not out of it.

Finally, the men and women of that early Church of which we are thinking were conscious of a joyous sense of deliverance, and what they felt themselves delivered from was bondage to the dictates of blind chance. It could be put another way by saying that they felt themselves delivered from that which is the scourge of our contemporary world perhaps more than anything else—meaninglessness, lack of motive and purpose. It has not been by accident that all down the ages some of the acutest minds have found meaning and purpose in Christ and His Church which they were acutely conscious of lacking in the unredeemed world. The sad pointlessness of so

[1] Colossians 3. 11.

much life which is cut off from the things of the Spirit, has been marvellously described by T. S. Eliot in *East Coker*:

O dark dark dark. They all go into the dark,
The vacant interstellar spaces, the vacant into the vacant,
The captains, merchant bankers, eminent men of letters,
The generous patrons of art, the statesmen and the rulers,
Distinguished civil servants, chairmen of many committees,
Industrial lords and petty contractors, all go into the dark.
And dark the sun and moon, and the Almanack de Gotha
And the Stock Exchange Gazette, the Directory of Directors,
    and cold the sense and lost the motive of action.
And we all go with them, into the silent funeral,
And nobody's funeral, for there is no-one to bury.
I said to my soul, be still, and let the dark come upon you
Which shall be the darkness of God. As, in a theatre,
The lights are extinguished, for the scene to be changed
With a hollow rumble of wings, with a movement of dark-
    ness on darkness.
And we know that the hills and the trees, the distant pano-
    rama
And the bold imposing facade are all being rolled away—
Or as, when an underground train, in the tube, stops too
    long between stations
And the conversation rises and slowly fades into silence
And you see behind every face the mental emptiness deepen
Leaving only the growing terror of nothing to think about.

Such, then, are some of the qualities which give life, meaning and purpose to a Christian faith which is Spirit-filled. No amount of re-deployment of its resources or of re-structuring of its organizations, obviously necessary as these things are to meet the demands of the changing world, can be of the slightest value unless that Church which is thus re-deployed and re-structured has the Spirit in it. But for those who feel, as many do now, that somehow the virtue has gone out of the faith they hold or would wish to hold, the constant and exciting possibility of themselves laying hold upon this Spirit in their own lives is at hand. For not only is the Holy Spirit a gift: the Holy Spirit is a gift which has already been given, and it remains for those to whom it has been given to lay hold upon it. But Christ through his Holy Spirit will not force himself upon us; rather will he wait for us to invite him into our lives and into our society. It is at that point, and at that point alone, that there lies the possibility of a Christian revival which may yet astonish the world, one that will bring back to that world through the lives of Spirit-filled Christian men and women a new experience of God, a new consciousness of the supernatural, a new sense of service to mankind, a new sense of hope in place of the current meaninglessness, a new colour, in fact, to a life which has grown grey. In many ways, we are all living through a winter of the spirit. And yet, such are the ways of God, that, as Shelley put it in another connection,

If Winter comes, can Spring be far behind?

8. Out Into the World

WHERE THEN does this leave us? What is the relevance of all this to the particular situation now of all those quiet people, as we have called them, to whom all this has been primarily addressed? There they are, struggling to be faithful to the faith as they see it, and in the form in which it has been mediated to them, in an era of violent change when almost every institution they have known, including the Church, stands in obvious need of restructuring in almost every particular. There they are, wide open to the temptation, as indeed we all are, of confusing changelessness of outer forms with the survival of inner truth, and therefore prone to feel desperately dismayed when the changes which are sweeping the world today catch up with things they have long held sacred. And yet there they are still, as we have tried to say previously, 'very important people in terms of the future of the Christian faith in this land, with all that that implies not only in personal lives, but as an influence upon the whole tone and nature of our society. They have always been in our society quietly holding up, like the solid pillars of some foundation which few visit, but which is essential to the safety of the building above, the values by which the majority still live. These values in the last resort depend upon the consciousness that human life has a larger dimension than the entirely material, and that men and women can be sustained by a larger hope and are answerable to a loftier judgement than any which this world affords.' The responsibility resting upon these, who make up the vast majority of today's Christians and who form an essential link between the present and tomorrow's Christians, of seeing that there shall be a Christian presence in society in the meantime, is heavy indeed. The relevance of all, therefore, that we have tried thus far to say lies in the area of the task which faces all of us nowadays of taking our faith more boldly, and with less inhibitions, out into the world than many of us have been accustomed to so far. The luxury of being reticent about what we believe is, surely, like many other luxuries, one that we can no longer afford, because the situation in which we are all called upon to make our witness now is one of the greatest possible gravity and urgency.

There have been many diagnoses made of the condition of our society today, and we have no intention whatever of adding to the number. That it is a deeply materialist society is obvious enough. Less obvious is the fact that it represents perhaps a first attempt to organize human life on the basis that God does not matter. It therefore follows that those who believe that he does have the challenge laid before them of demonstrating, by what they themselves are and by what they themselves do, that God does in fact matter, and matter enormously. The conviction here expressed is, however, that no witness of this sort which leaves out testimony to Christ as a person, or which is not warmed at its core by a sense of personal encounter with Christ, or which is not excited by the constant possibilities arising above the limitations of self in the power of the Holy Spirit, can ever have hope of being other than a dead thing. It was arising out of that conviction that we have tried to set forth what Christ has meant in our own lives for the very reason that those lives have been ordinary rather than extraordinary. And it was for the same reason that we tried to show forth a little of what we believe we have seen of him in the lives of others whom we have met.

We return now, then, to this task lying upon each one of us of taking our faith out into the world. That it is a world in which, to a considerable extent, the Church is unnecessary, redundant and irrelevant is a fact. In so far as this is true it is a judgement upon us all. We have all had a hand, after all, in making that Church which is, or should be, the instrument of God's purposes, so inadequate in these respects. Here is a passage, for instance, descriptive of the nineteenth-century Anglican Church in Britain which may well in some respects be a true picture of that same Church as some of us know it today.

'The supreme weakness was a failure to understand the signs of the times, a failure of vision and perception, stemming from theological error that narrowed the claims of God and the concern of the Church from the dimension of the Kingdom to the dimension of "religion." Inevitably it meant that the churches were preoccupied with their own affairs rather than with the affairs of the world; witness the tumultuous clamour on establishment and disestablishment, ritualism and Romanism, the controversies on education, Burial Acts and deceased wife's sister. A failure of prophesy always spells a failure of sensitivity. There was a lack of creative tension with contemporary thought, and the strong emphasis on personal morality that either ruled out the issue of social morality altogether, or restricted that concern to such social evils as patently issued in the most glaring personal vice. Howbeit unconsciously, it was all calculated to produce a spirituality within the churches that was pathologically religious or highly conventional, lacking in understanding, sympathy and sensitive encounter with the estranged world.'[1]

[1] E. R. Wickham, *Church and People in an Industrial City*, Lutterworth Press.

In so far, then, as that is true of the Church as any of us may know it, then, surely, the challenge to make our own contribution of new life, new faith and new conviction within it is all the greater. It is a fair question to ask, for instance, how far a tape recording of the proceedings of some church council we may know would stand up to the cold evaluation of a play-back when compared with the atmosphere evoked by that passage in Acts which, speaking of the earliest days of the Church, describes how 'they met constantly to hear the Apostles teach, and to share the common life, to break bread, and to pray. A sense of awe was everywhere. . . .'[1] Some such bodies do in fact at this moment show forth splendid qualities of spiritual energy and enterprise. New life and aware-ness is, in fact, present in the Church here and now, here and there. The pity of it is that the here and there is by no means everywhere, and that meanwhile the task of renewal of the Church grows ever more pressing. Obviously, renewal must mean a taking down and a rebuilding, in some cases even a sweeping away, of much that many have held dear. But no amount of re-structur-ing and rearranging, or even of talking about them, are likely to be effective in any way unless those concerned in the enterprise themselves have a Gospel and are prepared to take it out and speak of it in the world with authority and humility.

So renewal is the need, and the call comes to all of us to help on that process, never forgetting, none the less, that renewal must start with ourselves, in our own hearts and minds. Meanwhile, it may be observed that renewal does not involve, and should not be understood as

[1] Acts 2. 42.

involving, a destruction of the old so much as a re-creation of it. Nor does it involve, nor should it involve, an unnecessary denigration of the Church of the past. It is this denigration of a rich past and of the heritage which belongs to us all which has done not a little to discourage and dishearten those who have drawn much from that heritage and still do. After all, in other walks of life where renewal and reconstruction are taking place, neither unnecessary denigration nor unnecessary demolition are by sensible people taken as necessary. The reconstruction of our railway system, for instance, is not effected by tearing up all the tracks or by persuading all railwaymen that they are no longer necessary and have in any event made a mistake by ever becoming railwaymen! The task is best approached by removing some of the tracks, perhaps by building new ones, and in any event by keeping those involved with the undertaking convinced of the worthwhileness of their activities. The Church in this land has had a mighty past; under God it will have a mighty future in helping to save the souls of people who are rapidly losing them. Any wholesale devaluation of its past is as unnecessary as it is injurious.

The point was well made by two articles in the periodical *New Christian*. The first of which, writing of what it called the coming non-Church, looked with satisfaction to the coming of the day which need not, it was suggested, be far distant, when the Church as we know it will have entirely vanished away to be replaced by occasional worship in occasional places as the spirit moved those who wished—the number of whom, one gathered, was likely to be small indeed. The second article, in reply to the first, ended with a splendid passage which says

so well what we would ourselves like to say, that we
take leave to quote it in full:

'God is an almost lost secret, worship an almost dead art;
but the worship of God is something which for the health of
our souls and bodies we must somehow keep alive and re-
discover. There were black days in Israel when there was no
open vision, the Lord seemed to have withdrawn himself,
no prophets spoke and shrines were little used. But the river
still flowed beneath the soil and in good time burst forth
again. Nobody then considered it a sacred duty to seal up the
springs with cement and make an unreclaimable desert.
Will it be our privilege in this modern age, at the same time
as we are poisoning our songbirds, choking our seabirds,
eliminating our buttercups and daisies, bombarding our moon
with hardware and showering our soil with strontium-90,
to slam the door irrevocably on the God of our salvation in
whose will is our peace and without whom our souls must
wander restlessly in dry places?'[1]

When Father Basil Jellicoe, the founder of the St.
Pancras Housing Association, arrived in what was then
that slum area in the years immediately after the first
world war, and surveyed the appalling scene, the words
of Isaiah came into his mind: 'They shall rebuild the
old wastes, they shall raise up the former desolations, and
they shall repair the waste cities, the destruction of
many generations.' It is in a similar spirit, surely, that
we may best look to the task of the renewal of the Church
in our day.

But this renewal must involve the removal of those
sins and errors which are preventing the Church from
breaking out with power into the contemporary scene.
And this, beyond all else, must start with a renewed

[1] Alison Adcock in *New Christian*, July 14th, 1966.

encounter with Christ through the Holy Spirit. The sins
and errors are beyond all else those of being inward-
looking, of being concerned primarily with our own
affairs, and only peripherally with the needs of the world
and of the men and women in it. The power of the Holy
Spirit, which is God's gift to us, is always available, but
there can be no renewal unless in obedience and faith
and with a high sense of adventure we avail ourselves of it;
breaking out, in order to do so, from the hard shell of old
prejudice and from all those frozen attitudes of mind
under the influence of which we may be tempted to
believe that this is no longer an age of faith.

But what does this mean in practice? All through this
book we have deliberately confined ourselves, in such
illustrations as we have tried to give of the movement
of the Spirit in people's lives, to the small scale and
the localized. We have done so because we believe that
this is the way Christ works, coming to individuals as
once by Galilee, and moving them strangely in ways
which they know to be crucial, even though to the outside
observer they may seem small enough. Thus one of the
writers of this book, looking back to the days preceding
the consecration of Coventry Cathedral, recalls how, in
preparation for a mission to the diocese associated with
that event, it was his practice to call upon people to pray,
suggesting that some might be prepared to do so in an
extempore manner. Usually, such was the habitual
reticence of those who attended, there was little or no
response. But on one occasion, in a crowded parish hall
in the heart of the country, when the request was pressed
hard, a middle-aged woman—one of the quiet people if
ever there was one—rose to her feet. She prayed with
difficulty and with diffidence, and clearly with a costly

struggle. It was a thing she had never done before in her life, nor had ever dreamt of doing. Subsequently, she wrote to say that this little event had been a turning point in her life, and it is the fact that she has developed from that point into a fullness and joyousness of Christian service and leadership in her community of which before she would certainly not have been capable and to which indeed she would never have aspired. A small incident? A little local matter ludicrously small scale by comparison with the great events of the world? Possibly; but so was the call of Matthew, or Christ's talk with the fishermen. These were minute matters compared with what was going on in Jerusalem or Rome; but they conquered the world of Jerusalem and Rome, in the end.

The evidence suggests that there must have been many great movements of the Spirit—the revival under John Wesley which did so much to redeem the soul of eighteenth-century Britain is a case in point—which must have begun by incidents of this sort multiplied a thousand times. History tends in after times to formalize and de-personalize the account of what happened. But let it never be forgotten that the protagonists are God and people, and that God works upon people in this person to person manner, never being embarrassed, as some little men are, by what appears at the time to be small scale.

But he works with power, sometimes choosing to remind us of powers which he places within our reach, but which we have forgotten. This epoch may well be the midnight of institutional religion. That there will be a dawn, that, to change the metaphor, there will be a glorious summer after this winter of our discontent, is certain. Equally certain is that the dawn, when it comes, will reveal many changes. Meanwhile, the duty lies

upon all who have heard that Gospel, and to whom
Christ has come in one or other of the many ways in which
he does come into human lives, to speak more boldly, as
they ought to speak, of the faith that is in them.

One of the authors of this book, writing in his diocesan
newspaper at the conclusion of the 1966 Billy Graham
Campaign—a campaign which, predictably, drew much
criticism and of which he was well aware, and in some of
which he was in agreement—wrote none the less: 'We
can learn that there is a strong and widely-felt wistful
hunger for faith in the nation. Secondly, there is evidence
of a keen desire for preaching with authority, with
conviction and with power. Thirdly, there is a great
longing for preaching with a positive content—people are
getting rather tired of being told what they cannot
believe and are longing with all their hearts to be told
what they can believe. . . . We have seen, once again,
the compelling attraction of the person of Jesus Christ—
once again we have seen evidence of the statement "I, if I
be lifted up, will draw all men unto me."' Elsewhere
in that same paper there was reproduced the humble,
outwardly very modest programme which the evangelist
in his final meeting had urged upon all those who had
felt at all drawn by what he had to say. It included
reading the Bible every day, joining a prayer group,
being an effective member of a church, engaging in
active service for others, living by faith in Christ, exercising
personal discipline based on his life and teaching, and
believing his promise that he would give power to make
lives purposeful and creative, so that they could be forces
for good in the world.

From such humble self-dedication, always provided it
has been in the name of Christ, great things have come

in the long sweep of Christian history. There is no reason whatever for supposing that they will not come again. But all depends on Christ, and on personal commitment to him, as it always has. 'Here I stand knocking at the door,' says that mysterious message in the Book of Revelation, 'if anyone hears my voice and opens the door, I will come in and sit down to supper with him and he with me.'[1]

[1] Revelation 3. 20.